LOUIS B. WRIGHT, General Editor. Director of the Folger Shakespeare Library from 1948 until his retirement in 1968, Dr. Wright has devoted over forty years to the study of the Shakespearean period. In 1926 he completed his doctoral thesis on "Vaudeville Elements in Elizabethan Drama" and subsequently published many articles on the stagecraft and theatre of Shakespeare's day. He is the author of *Middle-Class Culture in Elizabethan England* (1935), *Religion and Empire* (1942), *The Elizabethans' America* (1965), and many other books and essays on the history and literature of the Tudor and Stuart periods, including *Shakespeare for Everyman* (1964). Dr. Wright has taught at the universities of North Carolina, California at Los Angeles, Michigan, Minnesota, and other American institutions. From 1932 to 1948 he was instrumental in developing the research program of the Henry E. Huntington Library and Art Gallery. During his tenure as Director, the Folger Shakespeare Library became one of the leading research institutions of the world for the study of the backgrounds of Anglo-American civilization.

VIRGINIA A. LaMAR, Assistant Editor. A member of the staff of the Folger Shakespeare Library from 1946 until her death in 1968, Miss LaMar served as research assistant to the Director and as Executive Secretary. Prior to 1946 Miss LaMar had been a secretary in the British Admiralty Delegation in Washington, D.C., receiving the King's Medal in 1945 for her services. She was coeditor of the *Historie of Travell into Virginia Britania* by William Strachey, published by The Hakluyt Society in 1953, and author of *English Dress in the Age of Shakespeare* and *Travel and Roads in England* in the "Folger Booklets on Tudor and Stuart Civilization" series.

The Folger Shakespeare Library

GENERAL EDITOR
LOUIS B. WRIGHT
Director, Folger Shakespeare Library, 1948–1968

•

ASSISTANT EDITOR
VIRGINIA A. LaMAR
Executive Secretary, Folger Shakespeare Library, 1946–1968

The Folger Library General Reader's Shakespeare

SHAKESPEARE'S
SONNETS

WASHINGTON SQUARE PRESS
POCKET BOOKS • NEW YORK

SHAKESPEARE'S SONNETS

WASHINGTON SQUARE PRESS edition published October, 1967
5th printing.....................December, 1976

A new edition of a distinguished
literary work now made available in
an inexpensive, well-designed format

Published by
POCKET BOOKS, a division of Simon & Schuster, Inc.,
A GULF+WESTERN COMPANY
630 Fifth Avenue, New York, N.Y. 10020.

WASHINGTON SQUARE PRESS editions are distrib-
uted in the U.S. by Simon & Schuster, Inc., 630 Fifth
Avenue, New York, N.Y. 10020, and in Canada by Simon
& Schuster of Canada, Ltd., Markham, Ontario, Canada.

ISBN: 0-671-48804-X.

Preface

This edition of Shakespeare's *Sonnets* is designed to make available the text of a collection of poems that are the most personal of any of Shakespeare's works and contain some of the world's greatest love poetry. In the centuries since Shakespeare, many changes have occurred in the meanings of words, which makes clarification of Shakespeare's vocabulary desirable. Writing in the sonnet form also resulted in even greater compression of meaning than is found in blank verse. In the notes, placed opposite the sonnet they explain, we have tried to suggest multiple meanings, as well as to give synonyms for single words. In addition, beneath the notes we have supplied a brief prose paraphrase for each sonnet, giving our interpretation of its fundamental meaning. Readers who wish to study the sonnets more intensively should see the References for Further Reading for additional titles on the subject.

L. B. W.
V. A. L.

September 15, 1966

In 1609 Thomas Thorpe, a London publisher, brought out a small quarto volume described on the title page as *Shakespeare's Sonnets. Never before Imprinted.* There is no evidence that Shakespeare himself had anything to do with the publication of

SHAKE-SPEARES

SONNETS

Neuer before Imprinted.

———————————

———————————

AT LONDON
By *G. Eld* for *T. T.* and are
to be solde by *william Aspley.*
1609.

The title page of the 1609 Quarto of the *Sonnets.*

these poems; the number of misprints and the illogical punctuation indicate that the author did not see the book through the press.

Since the late eighteenth century, Shakespeare's sonnets have excited the interest of scholars and fascinated readers of poetry. The English critic and literary historian C. S. Lewis has declared that in the English tradition Shakespeare in the sonnets has shown himself to be the supreme poet of love. The sonnets stir interest not only because of their poetic appeal but because they are wrapped in mystery. Hundreds of books and thousands of articles have been written in England, the United States, Germany, France, and elsewhere trying to unravel a puzzle that continually stimulates scholarly curiosity. We would like to settle once and for all the identity of Mr. W. H., "the only begetter," to whom the first published edition of the sonnets is dedicated; we would like to know the name of the male friend to whom most of the poems are addressed; we would also like to identify the rival poet, mentioned in some of the sonnets, and the author's mistress, the "dark lady," for whom he expressed both love and hatred. These puzzles have produced a vast outpouring of books and essays, not one of which can offer conclusive proof, however completely their authors may have convinced themselves.

Sir Edmund Chambers, commenting upon the wide variety of interpretations of the sonnets, observes: "There is room for subjective interpretations; and the licence has been freely used. It has been held that the sonnets of the main series were not all written to the same person; that some of them were after all to a woman, [Queen] Elizabeth or Anne Hathaway or another; that they were written for another man to give to a woman, or for a woman to give to a man; that their intention is dramatic and not personal; that they are a dialogue between 'You' and 'Thou'; that they are allegorical; that they are merely literary exercises in the Petrarchan convention. There is much absurdity in many of these views. More folly has been written about the sonnets than about any other Shakespearean topic" (*William Shakespeare*, I, 560-561).

Considering the oceans of nonsense written about other topics in Shakespeare, Sir Edmund's categorical statement should serve as a warning to those who would swallow whole any interpretation of the sonnets. Indeed, anyone, scholar or casual reader, who gets a burst of light that reveals to him the solution of the problems of the sonnets should read carefully and prayerfully Volume II of *A New Variorum Edition of Shakespeare: The Sonnets*, edited by Hyder E. Rollins (Philadelphia, 1944). The chances are that the reader will discover that his solution or interpretation has been anticipated, sometimes many times over, during past decades. Few volumes contain more evidence of misplaced ingenuity than Rollins' summaries of the interpretations of the sonnets. His own judicious commentaries upon the various views should be given the consideration they deserve.

A reader of the sonnets should be warned that conservative scholars take an agnostic attitude toward all of the pat solutions of the mysteries that the poems suggest. No proof at present exists as to the identity of Mr. W. H., the male friend addressed in many of the sonnets, the rival poet, or the dark lady. Furthermore, unless some new document turns up, some letter or hitherto unknown statement by Shakespeare or a contemporary, no definitive solution of these mysteries can be expected.

Nevertheless, critics and editors of the sonnets continually press forward with "solutions." Some of these speak with infinite assurance. For example, Professor A. L. Rowse, in an edition of the sonnets in 1964, has dusted off the old theory that the Earl of Southampton is the "friend," and, using his own prestige as an historian, has convinced himself of this identity, which he sets forth as proved truth.

Not to be put down by an historian, Professor John Dover Wilson, editor of the Cambridge Shakespeare, replied to Professor Rowse in the same year with a brilliant little volume, *An Introduction to the Sonnets of Shakespeare for the Use of Historians and Others,* in which he refuted the notion that Southampton was the friend and once more set forth arguments for the identity of William Herbert, third Earl of Pembroke, as the friend. In this debate, Professor Wilson appears to have the edge on Professor Rowse. In the course of the years, scores of scholars have espoused the cause of Southampton and of Pembroke, the two leading contenders among a number of candidates for the friend. In some instances, a scholar has switched his allegiance from Southampton to Pembroke, or vice versa. For instance, Sir Sidney Lee at first argued for Pembroke but later changed sides, recanted his former views, condemned the Pembrokists, and "discovered" that Southampton was the friend.

During the past few years, Pembroke's star has been rising, and many critics appear to believe that the facts of Pembroke's life, particularly his age, consort better with internal evidence in the sonnets than do the details of Southampton's life. The case for Southampton as the friend is based primarily on the fact that Shakespeare dedicated to him *Venus and Adonis* and *The Rape of Lucrece,* in the hope, perhaps, that Southampton would become his patron. But proof is lacking that Southampton actually was Shakespeare's patron. As the friend in the sonnets, Southampton's age poses some difficulties. He was born in 1573, which makes him nearer in age to the poet than the sonnets to the friend suggest and would necessitate a date of composition in the 1580's (before sonnet writing was at the height of its popularity). Otherwise he could not plausibly be called a "lovely boy." Pembroke, who was born in 1580, is of a more satisfactory age, if the "procreation" sonnets were written about 1595, when Pembroke's parents began their unsuccessful efforts to arrange a suitable marriage for their young son; he did not finally marry until 1604. Although Shakespeare dedicated his narrative poems to Southampton, Heminges and Condell dedicated the First Folio to Pembroke and his brother and mentioned the favor shown by them to the playwright during his lifetime. Pembroke and his mother were noted patrons of literature and the arts; Southampton showed more interest in politics. But the truth is that all of this is pure speculation and no certain identification can be made.

Like the problem of the friend, the question of the identities of Mr. W. H., the rival poet, and the dark lady has produced a vast amount of speculation but no convincing proof. Christopher Marlowe, George Chapman, Samuel Daniel, and others have advocates for the part of rival poet. Even Dante and Tasso, curiously, have been mentioned for this honor. The dark lady was once thought to be Mary Fitton, one of Queen Elizabeth's maids of honor, who for a time was mistress to Pembroke and bore him a son in March, 1601. But portraits of her turned up which revealed that she was neither brunette nor dark-eyed.

The question of Mr. W. H. is complicated by the interpretation of the statement in the dedication of the 1609 quarto describing him as the "only begetter" of the sonnets. Nobody knows the source of the copy that the publisher, Thomas Thorpe, sent to the printer in 1609. But the published volume bore a dedication, signed by Thorpe's initials, "To the only begetter of these ensuing sonnets, Mr. W. H." Whether Thorpe meant to compliment someone who procured the copy for the sonnets, or to imply that W. H. had been the inspiration of the author, is anybody's guess, and many guesses have found their way into print. "Master W. H., the only begetter of the foregoing sonnets, has caused the spilling of more ink, the utterance of more futile words, than almost any other personage or problem of Q [Quarto 1], and there is not the slightest likelihood that the mystery surrounding his initials will ever be dispelled in a fashion satisfactory to a majority of critics, editors, and commentators," Rollins comments (II, 166).

Besides the mere fascination that comes from a beguiling mystery, the solution of these problems has interested students of Shakespeare because the sonnets may be autobiographical, and any clue to Shakespeare's life and personality is eagerly pursued. Long ago the poet Wordsworth said of the sonnets that "with this key Shakespeare unlocked his heart." But not everyone agrees that the sonnets are a revelation of the author's life. Some scholars believe that they are Shakespeare's contribution to a literary form that was fashionable at the moment and are not to be taken literally as genuine expressions of the poet's own emotions. Of this school of thought, Rollins remarks that "the literary exercise—or at least the non-autobiographical—theory has increased in favor till its proponents almost outnumber those of the personal theory" (II, 152).

On the chameleon-like character of the poet, the words of John Keats, another poet, who greatly admired Shakespeare, may be worth quoting: "As to the poetical Character itself . . . it is not itself—it has no self—It has no character. . . . A poet is the most unpoetical of any thing in existence; because he has no Identity—he is continually informing and filling some other Body" (quoted in J. B. Leishman, *Themes and Variations in Shakespeare's Sonnets*, p. 127, from Keats's letter to Richard Woodhouse, October 27, 1818).

Although it is hard to believe that some of these emotion-packed verses are not self-revelations, critics point out that Shakespeare "was capable of profound and passionate utterance under the impulse of imagination alone." Whether the author was revealing the agonies that he suffered or the joy that he experienced from his friendship with some highborn nobleman, or whether he confessed some real love affair with a mistress who at times held a hypnotic attraction and at other times repelled him, we shall never know.

We do not even know whether the order in which Thorpe had the sonnets printed was the author's own arrangement. Some scholars have tried rearranging the sonnets to make them tell a more connected story and to fit better into an autobiographical plan. Nearly everyone agrees that Shakespeare had nothing to do with Thorpe's publication; that the sonnets were obtained surreptitiously and printed without the author's knowledge.

The date of composition of the sonnets is also uncertain. Obviously they were written sometime before early 1609, when Thorpe had the first edition printed. But as early as 1598, in *Palladis Tamia*, Francis Meres had written that "the sweet witty soul of Ovid lives in mellifluous and honey-tongued Shakespeare, witness his *Venus and Adonis*, his *Lucrece*, his sugared sonnets among his private friends." Yet no one knows whether the printed sonnets are the "sugared" verses that Meres mentioned. Two of the sonnets, Nos. 138 and 144, had been printed in 1599 in a collection of verse entitled *The Passionate Pilgrim*. After surveying all the evidence for the date of composition, Rollins concludes: "An average of the guesses indicates that

Sh. began writing about the middle of 1593 and laid aside his pen about June, 1599. Perhaps such an average is as reliable a way as has yet been found of 'settling' the vexed problem. . . . In any case, it should be unnecessary to say here that the date of composition is altogether doubtful" (II, 73).

Since the sonnets addressed to a man are frequently expressed in terms of romantic love, readers have raised the question of whether Shakespeare reveals in them a homosexual attachment to his friend and patron. Even if the sonnets are autobiographical, psychological interpreters have pointed out that certain of them clearly signify that the writer was not a homosexual. The first seventeen sonnets, for example, urge the friend and patron to marry and beget children. "No homosexual would ever urge such action," one writer quoted by Rollins declares (II, 239). The consensus of those who have pondered this problem is that Shakespeare's love was not abnormal and that his expressions merely follow Renaissance conventions and terminology.

Many scholars have searched for sources of Shakespeare's sonnets, but they have found almost no direct borrowings from others. Shakespeare found in Ovid conventional expressions used in love lyrics by poets from Ovid's time onward. Other conventional ideas and phrases common among the sonneteers frequently appear in Shakespeare's verse, but they do not indicate indebtedness to any particular contemporary. We have illustrated some of the sonnets with pictures and verses from an emblem book, the *Amorum emblemata* of Octavio van Veen (Antwerp, 1608). The similarity of ideas between this book and the sonnets merely proves that, however original may have been Shakespeare's expression, he drew upon many commonplaces in the conceits used in his love poetry.

Sonnets are not an indigenous English poetic form. They were imported from Italy, sometimes via France. Petrarch was the great Renaissance inspiration of sonneteering, for his sonnets to Laura

Petrarch. From *Il Petrarca con l'espositione d'Alessandro Vellutello* (1538).

were widely read, translated, and imitated throughout western Europe. Other Italian writers, of course, employed the sonnet form—Dante, Tasso, Ariosto, Michelangelo—but Petrarch was the primary influence in spreading the type abroad. The typical Italian sonnet was fourteen lines long: the first eight lines—the octave—introduced the theme, and the last six lines—the sestet—gave the conclusion. The rhyme scheme of the octave was normally *abba, abba,* or *abba, acca;* and the sestet normally rhymed *cdecde, cdcdcd,* or *cdcdee.*

Shakespeare employed a slightly different form for his sonnets. Most of Shakespeare's sonnets consist of three quatrains with alternate rhyme and a concluding couplet. The usual line is iambic pen-

Torquato Tasso, one of the Italian exponents of the love sonnet. From Tasso's *Gierusalemme liberata* (1724).

tameter, that is, ten syllables with the stress on the second of each pair of syllables. Not all of Shakespeare's contemporaries used his precise form. Edmund Spenser, for example, wrote sonnets rhyming *abab, bcbc, cdcd, ee.* Some poems called sonnets had only twelve lines, and a few had more than fourteen lines. Early in the Tudor period, the term sonnet was sometimes used for almost any type of short poem on a single theme.

The first work to popularize the sonnet by name was published by a printer named Richard Tottel in 1557 as *Songs and Sonnets.* It was a miscellany containing work by early Tudor poets, with imitations and translations from Petrarch. Extremely popular, this miscellany went through at least nine editions by 1587 and helped to stimulate a vogue for the sonnet, which became a highly fashionable form of verse in the 1590's. The first important sonnet sequence was Sir Philip Sidney's *Astrophel and Stella,* published in 1591. During the following decade, every significant poet felt impelled to write sonnets. Some of the more important cycles are Samuel Daniel's *Delia* (1592), Henry Constable's *Diana* (1592), Thomas Watson's, *The Tears of Fancy, or Love Disdained* (1593), Thomas Lodge's *Phillis* (1593), Michael Drayton's *Idea's Mirror* (1594), and Edmund Spenser's *Amoretti* (1595). The title of Drayton's sequence was apparently meant to suggest that it was merely a literary exercise.

Since we cannot be certain that Shakespeare's sonnets were intended to be a continuous autobiographical revelation, we shall make a mistake if we try to read them as we would a novel—for the story

PETRVS RONSARDVS VINDOMIESIS POE GAL

Byfonij cecenit Uates ad Strymonis undas
Non melius, tibj quam funditur ore melos.

Pierre Ronsard. From Jean Jacques Boissard, *Icones virorum illustrium* (1597).

that they disclose. Many readers, in fact, will find
their greatest satisfaction in reading the sonnets out
of context, that is, as individual poetic units. Even
though we may disregard the person or persons to
whom the sonnets may have been addressed, as individual poems they are often supreme expressions
of some phase of man's relation to life: love, hope,
fear, weariness, despair—almost any mood reflected
in man's emotions. Frequently we feel that in the
main portion of the sonnet the author is expressing
some profound thought but feels impelled by the
convention of the form to tie it to a meaning in the
concluding couplet that the preceding verses only
vaguely suggest. We can enjoy many of the son-

ₙₑ₋ by disregarding the tag lines at the end. In fact, the lines most often quoted from the sonnets often stop short of the conclusion.

We need no "story element" to give us an appreciation of No. 73, which, like others of Shakespeare's sonnets, laments the ravages of Time:

> That time of year thou mayst in me behold
> When yellow leaves, or none, or few, do hang
> Upon those boughs which shake against the cold,
> Bare, ruined choirs where late the sweet birds sang.

These four lines, compact and full of meaning, have rarely been equalled for their evocative quality, the pictures they call up, the mood they induce. Equally famous is another lament, No. 30, on the losses brought by time:

> When to the sessions of sweet silent thought
> I summon up remembrance of things past,
> I sigh the lack of many a thing I sought,
> And with old woes new wail my dear time's waste.

A similar but even more melancholy mood is stressed in No. 64:

> When I have seen by Time's fell hand defaced
> The rich, proud cost of outworn buried age,
> When sometime lofty towers I see down-rased
> And brass eternal slave to mortal rage;
>
> . . . .
>
> This thought is as a death, which cannot choose
> But weep to have that which it fears to lose.

Only the immortality conferred by poetry can compensate for the devastations wrought by Time, Shakespeare assures his patron in No. 55:

> Not marble nor the gilded monuments
> Of princes shall outlive this pow'rful rhyme,
> But you shall shine more bright in these contents
> Than unswept stone, besmeared with sluttish time.

The reader of one of the most famous sonnets, No. 116, need not care whether it is addressed to the author's patron or to some unknown woman. Its expression of fidelity has become immortal:

> Let me not to the marriage of true minds
> Admit impediments; love is not love
> Which alters when it alteration finds,
>
> . . . .
>
> Love alters not with his brief hours and weeks,
> But bears it out even to the edge of Doom.
>   If this be error, and upon me proved,
>   I never writ, nor no man ever loved.

Some of the sonnets please us by the sheer exuberance of their imagery. Even when Shakespeare employs conventional tropes common to the sonnet cycles, he gives them a freshness and a vitality that makes them savor of originality. For example, any traveller who has journeyed through Warwickshire with sun and cloud can believe that Shakespeare in No. 33 was writing from remembered experience:

Full many a glorious morning have I seen
Flatter the mountaintops with sovereign eye,
Kissing with golden face the meadows green,
Gilding pale streams with heavenly alchemy.

In similar fashion, the imagery of No. 98 reflects a direct response to the beauty of nature, not the conventions of the sonnet form:

From you have I been absent in the spring,
When proud-pied April, dressed in all his trim,
Hath put a spirit of youth in everything,
That heavy Saturn laughed and leapt with him.

Although the most famous of the sonnets deal with themes of melancholy, the sonnets are not devoid of humor, even humor at the expense of his putative mistress. In No. 130, he satirizes, if not his mistress, at least the conventions of sonneteers who usually described their loves as blondes with hair "like golden wires." He will have none of this:

My mistress' eyes are nothing like the sun;
Coral is far more red than her lips' red;
If snow be white, why then her breasts are dun;
If hairs be wires, black wires grow on her head.

The greatest enjoyment of Shakespeare's sonnets will come from reading them as individual poems rather than from treating them as riddles to be solved. These riddles have defied the ingenuity of embattled scholars for centuries, and the intrusion of inexplicable autobiography can spoil the impact of verse that ought to please by its imagery no less than by its thought.

Shakespeare's sonnets in his own time were apparently far less popular than his two narrative poems, *Venus and Adonis* (1593), which had fourteen quarto editions before 1640, and *The Rape of Lucrece* (1594), which had seven quarto editions before 1640. The sonnets had no printing after 1609 until 1640, when a bookseller named John Benson put together a volume containing sonnets pirated from Thorpe's edition of 1609 and with additional poems by a dozen or more different authors. Benson's book appeared bearing the title *Poems: Written by Wil. Shake-Speare. Gent.* Benson rearranged the sonnets, changed some of them to refer to a woman instead of a man, and left out a few. His version has no textual validity and merely reprints, with added errors, most of the sonnets in Thorpe's edition. Nevertheless, many eighteenth-century editions of Shakespeare's sonnets were based on Benson's *Poems.* The last edition of Shakespeare to use Benson's text was apparently that published in New York in 1817-18 by Henry Durrell.

The 1609 edition by Thorpe is the only version having any textual authority. It contains many misprints, and later editors have had to make needed emendations.

The reputation and popularity of Shakespeare's sonnets have fluctuated from time to time and place to place. During the later seventeenth and early eighteenth centuries they were virtually ignored. The early editors of Shakespeare did not bother to include the sonnets among his works. Nicholas

Rowe, the first modern editor, for example, confined his edition to the plays. Alexander Pope followed Rowe's practice in the 1723-25 edition, but George Sewell, in 1725, brought out a supplement to include the narrative poems and sonnets.

So late as 1793, George Steevens, in the preface to his edition of Shakespeare, commented concerning the sonnets: "We have not reprinted the Sonnets, &c. of Shakespeare because the strongest act of Parliament that could be framed would fail to compel readers into their service. . . . Had Shakespeare produced no other works than these, his name would have reached us with as little celebrity as time has conferred on that of Thomas Watson, an older and much more elegant sonneteer." Rollins points out that Steevens was expressing the general opinion of his age about the sonnets. Although eighteenth-century poets occasionally used the sonnet form, this type of verse was not popular; the dislike of the age for this form of verse helps to explain the lack of interest in Shakespeare's sonnets.

During the late years of the eighteenth and the early nineteenth centuries, romantic poets began to employ the sonnet form again. Shakespeare's sonnets were "rediscovered," and from the third quarter of the nineteenth century they began to increase in popularity. The "mystery" of Shakespeare's sonnets excited scholars in England, Germany, and the United States, and research into the "problems" of the sonnets stimulated further interest. Since the mid-nineteenth century literally hundreds of editions of the sonnets have appeared, and the end is not in sight. Any printer who wants to bring out a handsome contribution to fine typography can be sure of a sale if he decides to reproduce the text of Shakespeare's sonnets. Few works today are more popular or more widely distributed than the sonnets.

THE AUTHOR

As early as 1598 Shakespeare was so well known as a literary and dramatic craftsman that Francis Meres, in his *Palladis Tamia: Wits Treasury,* referred in flattering terms to him as "mellifluous and honey-tongued Shakespeare," famous for his *Venus and Adonis,* his *Lucrece,* and "his sugared sonnets," which were circulating "among his private friends." Meres observes further that "as Plautus and Seneca are accounted the best for comedy and tragedy among the Latins, so Shakespeare among the English is the most excellent in both kinds for the stage," and he mentions a dozen plays that had made a name for Shakespeare. He concludes with the remark that "the Muses would speak with Shakespeare's fine filed phrase if they would speak English."

To those acquainted with the history of the Elizabethan and Jacobean periods, it is incredible that anyone should be so naïve or ignorant as to doubt the reality of Shakespeare as the author of the plays that bear his name. Yet so much nonsense has been written about other "candidates" for the plays that it is well to remind readers that no credible evidence that would stand up in a court of law has ever been adduced to prove either that Shakespeare did not write his plays or that anyone else wrote them. All the theories offered for the authorship of Francis Bacon, the Earl of Derby, the Earl of Oxford, the Earl of Hertford, Christopher Marlowe, and a score of other candidates are mere conjectures spun from the active imaginations of persons who confuse hypothesis and conjecture with evidence.

As Meres's statement of 1598 indicates, Shakespeare was already a popular playwright whose name carried weight at the box office. The obvious reputation of Shakespeare as early as 1598 makes the effort to prove him a myth one of the most absurd in the history of human perversity.

The anti-Shakespeareans talk darkly about a plot of vested interests to maintain the authorship of Shakespeare. Nobody has any vested interest in Shakespeare, but every scholar is interested in the truth and in the quality of evidence advanced by special pleaders who set forth hypotheses in place of facts.

The anti-Shakespeareans base their arguments upon a few simple premises, all of them false. These false premises are that Shakespeare was an unlettered yokel without any schooling, that nothing is known about Shakespeare, and that only a noble lord or the equivalent in background could have written the plays. The facts are that more is known about Shakespeare than about most dramatists of his day, that he had a very good education, acquired in the Stratford Grammar School, that the plays show no evidence of profound book learning, and that the knowledge of kings and courts evident in the plays is no greater than any intelligent young man could have picked up at second hand. Most anti-Shakespeareans are naïve and betray an obvious snobbery. The author of their favorite plays, they imply, must have had a college diploma framed and hung on his study wall like the one in their dentist's office, and obviously so great a writer must have had a title or some equally significant evidence of exalted social background. They forget that genius has a way of cropping up in unexpected places and that none of the great creative writers of the world got his inspiration in a college or university course.

William Shakespeare was the son of John Shakespeare of Stratford-upon-Avon, a substantial citizen of that small but busy market town in the center of the rich agricultural county of Warwick. John Shakespeare kept a shop, what we would call a general store; he dealt in wool and other produce and gradually acquired property. As a youth, John Shakespeare had learned the trade of glover and leather worker. There is no contemporary evidence that the elder Shakespeare was a butcher, though the anti-Shakespeareans like to talk about the ignorant "butcher's boy of Stratford." Their only evidence is a statement by gossipy John Aubrey, more than a century after William Shakespeare's birth, that young William followed his father's trade, and when he killed a calf, "he would do it in a high style and make a speech." We would like to believe the story true, but Aubrey is not a very credible witness.

John Shakespeare probably continued to operate

a farm at Snitterfield that his father had leased. He married Mary Arden, daughter of his father's landlord, a man of some property. The third of their eight children was William, baptized on April 26, 1564, and probably born three days before. At least, it is conventional to celebrate April 23 as his birthday.

The Stratford records give considerable information about John Shakespeare. We know that he held several municipal offices including those of alderman and mayor. In 1580 he was in some sort of legal difficulty and was fined for neglecting a summons of the Court of Queen's Bench requiring him to appear at Westminster and be bound over to keep the peace.

As a citizen and alderman of Stratford, John Shakespeare was entitled to send his son to the grammar school free. Though the records are lost, there can be no reason to doubt that this is where young William received his education. As any student of the period knows, the grammar schools provided the basic education in Latin learning and literature. The Elizabethan grammar school is not to be confused with modern grammar schools. Many cultivated men of the day received all their formal education in the grammar schools. At the universities in this period a student would have received little training that would have inspired him to be a creative writer. At Stratford young Shakespeare would have acquired a familiarity with Latin and some little knowledge of Greek. He would have read Latin authors and become acquainted with the plays of Plautus and Terence. Undoubtedly, in this period of his life he received that stimulation to read and explore for himself the world of ancient and modern history which he later utilized in his plays. The youngster who does not acquire this type of intellectual curiosity *before* college days rarely develops as a result of a college course the kind of mind Shakespeare demonstrated. His learning in books was anything but profound, but he clearly had the probing curiosity that sent him in search of information, and he had a keenness in the observation of nature and of humankind that finds reflection in his poetry.

There is little documentation for Shakespeare's boyhood. There is little reason why there should be. Nobody knew that he was going to be a dramatist about whom any scrap of information would be prized in the centuries to come. He was merely an active and vigorous youth of Stratford, perhaps assisting his father in his business, and no Boswell bothered to write down facts about him. The most important record that we have is a marriage license issued by the Bishop of Worcester on November 27, 1582, to permit William Shakespeare to marry Anne Hathaway, seven or eight years his senior; furthermore, the Bishop permitted the marriage after reading the banns only once instead of three times, evidence of the desire for haste. The need was explained on May 26, 1583, when the christening of Susanna, daughter of William and Anne Shakespeare, was recorded at Stratford. Two years later, on February 2, 1585, the records show the birth of twins to the Shakespeares, a boy and a girl who were christened Hamnet and Judith.

What William Shakespeare was doing in Stratford during the early years of his married life, or when he went to London, we do not know. It has been conjectured that he tried his hand at schoolteaching, but that is a mere guess. There is a legend that he left Stratford to escape a charge of poaching in the park of Sir Thomas Lucy of Charlecote, but there is no proof of this. There is also a legend that when first he came to London he earned his living by holding horses outside a playhouse and presently was given employment inside, but there is nothing better than eighteenth-century hearsay for this. How Shakespeare broke into the London theatres as a dramatist and actor we do not know. But lack of information is not surprising, for Elizabethans did not write their autobiographies, and we know even less about the lives of many writers and some men of affairs than we know about Shakespeare. By 1592 he was so well established and popular that he incurred the envy of the dramatist and pamphleteer Robert Greene, who referred to him as an "upstart crow . . . in his own conceit the only Shake-scene in a country." From this time onward, contemporary allusions and references in legal documents enable the scholar to chart Shakespeare's career with greater accuracy than is possible with most other Elizabethan dramatists.

By 1594 Shakespeare was a member of the company of actors known as the Lord Chamberlain's Men. After the accession of James I, in 1603, the company would have the sovereign for their patron and would be known as the King's Men. During the period of its greatest prosperity, this company would have as its principal theatres the Globe and the Blackfriars. Shakespeare was both an actor and a shareholder in the company. Tradition has assigned him such acting roles as Adam in *As You Like It* and the Ghost in *Hamlet,* a modest place on the stage that suggests that he may have had other duties in the management of the company. Such conclusions, however, are based on surmise.

What we do know is that his plays were popular and that he was highly successful in his vocation. His first play may have been *The Comedy of Errors,* acted perhaps in 1591. Certainly this was one of his earliest plays. The three parts of *Henry VI* were acted sometime between 1590 and 1592. Critics are not in agreement about precisely how much Shakespeare wrote of these three plays. *Richard III* probably dates from 1593. With this play Shakespeare captured the imagination of Elizabethan audiences, then enormously interested in historical plays. With *Richard III* Shakespeare also gave an interpretation pleasing to the Tudors of the rise to power of the grandfather of Queen Elizabeth. From this time onward, Shakespeare's plays followed on the stage in rapid succession: *Titus Andronicus, The Taming of the Shrew, The Two Gentlemen of Verona, Love's Labor's Lost, Romeo and Juliet, Richard II, A Midsummer Night's Dream, King John, The Merchant of Venice, Henry IV (Parts 1 and 2), Much Ado about Nothing, Henry V, Julius Caesar, As You Like It, Twelfth Night, Hamlet, The Merry Wives of Windsor, All's Well That Ends Well, Measure for Measure, Othello, King Lear,* and nine others that followed before Shakespeare retired completely, about 1613.

In the course of his career in London, he made enough money to enable him to retire to Stratford with a competence. His purchase on May 4, 1597, of New Place, then the second-largest dwelling in Stratford, "a pretty house of brick and timber," with a handsome garden, indicates his increasing prosperity. There his wife and children lived while he busied himself in the London theatres. The summer before he acquired New Place, his life was darkened by the death of his only son, Hamnet, a child of eleven. In May, 1602, Shakespeare purchased one hundred and seven acres of fertile farmland near Stratford and a few months later bought a cottage and garden across the alley from New Place. About 1611, he seems to have returned permanently to Stratford, for the next year a legal document refers to him as "William Shakespeare of Stratford-upon-Avon . . . gentleman." To achieve the desired appellation of gentleman, William Shakespeare had seen to it that the College of Heralds in 1596 granted his father a coat of arms. In one step he thus became a second-generation gentleman.

Shakespeare's daughter Susanna made a good match in 1607 with Dr. John Hall, a prominent and prosperous Stratford physician. His second daughter, Judith, did not marry until she was thirty-one years old, and then, under somewhat scandalous circumstances, she married Thomas Quiney, a Stratford vintner. On March 25, 1616, Shakespeare made his will, bequeathing his landed property to Susanna,

£300 to Judith, certain sums to other relatives, and his second-best bed to his wife, Anne. Much has been made of the second-best bed, but the legacy probably indicates only that Anne liked that particular bed. Shakespeare, following the practice of the time, may have already arranged with Susanna for his wife's care. Finally, on April 23, 1616, the anniversary of his birth, William Shakespeare died, and he was buried on April 25 within the chancel of Trinity Church, as befitted an honored citizen. On August 6, 1623, a few months before the publication of the collected edition of Shakespeare's plays, Anne Shakespeare joined her husband in death.

THE PUBLICATION OF HIS PLAYS

During his lifetime Shakespeare made no effort to publish any of his plays, though eighteen appeared in print in single-play editions known as quartos. Some of these are corrupt versions known as "bad quartos." No quarto, so far as is known, had the author's approval. Plays were not considered "literature" any more than most radio and television scripts today are considered literature. Dramatists sold their plays outright to the theatrical companies and it was usually considered in the company's interest to keep plays from getting into print. To achieve a reputation as a man of letters, Shakespeare wrote his *Sonnets* and his narrative poems, *Venus and Adonis* and *The Rape of Lucrece*, but he probably never dreamed that his plays would establish his reputation as a literary genius. Only Ben Jonson, a man known for his colossal conceit, had the crust to call his plays *Works,* as he did when he published an edition in 1616. But men laughed at Ben Jonson.

After Shakespeare's death, two of his old colleagues in the King's Men, John Heminges and Henry Condell, decided that it would be a good thing to print, in more accurate versions than were then available, the plays already published and eighteen additional plays not previously published in quarto. In 1623 appeared *Mr. William Shakespeares Comedies, Histories & Tragedies. Published according to the True Originall Copies. London. Printed by Isaac Iaggard and Ed. Blount.* This was the famous First Folio, a work that had the authority of Shakespeare's associates. The only play commonly attributed to Shakespeare that was omitted in the First Folio was *Pericles.* In their preface, "To the great Variety of Readers," Heminges and Condell state that whereas "you were abused with diverse stolen and surreptitious copies, maimed and deformed by the frauds and stealths of injurious impostors that exposed them, even those are now offered to your view cured and perfect of their limbs; and all the rest, absolute in their numbers, as he conceived them." What they used for printer's copy is one of the vexed problems of scholarship, and skilled bibliographers have devoted years of study to the question of the relation of the "copy" for the First Folio to Shakespeare's manuscripts. In some cases it is clear that the editors corrected printed quarto versions of the plays, probably by comparison with playhouse scripts. Whether these scripts were in Shakespeare's autograph is anybody's guess. No manuscript of any play in Shakespeare's handwriting has survived. Indeed, very few play manuscripts from this period by any author are extant. The Tudor and Stuart periods had not yet learned to prize autographs and authors' original manuscripts.

Since the First Folio contains eighteen plays not previously printed, it is the only source for these. For the other eighteen, which had appeared in quarto versions, the First Folio also has the authority of an edition prepared and overseen by Shakespeare's colleagues and professional associates. But since editorial standards in 1623 were far from strict, and Heminges and Condell were actors rather than editors by profession, the texts are sometimes careless. The printing and proofreading of the First Folio also left much to be desired, and some garbled passages have had to be corrected and emended. The "good quarto" texts have to be taken into account in preparing a modern edition.

Because of the great popularity of Shakespeare through the centuries, the First Folio has become a prized book, but it is not a very rare one, for it is estimated that 238 copies are extant. The Folger Shakespeare Library in Washington, D.C., has seventy-nine copies of the First Folio, collected by the founder, Henry Clay Folger, who believed that a collation of as many texts as possible would reveal significant facts about the text of Shakespeare's plays. Dr. Charlton Hinman, using an ingenious machine of his own invention for mechanical collating, has made many discoveries that throw light on Shakespeare's text and on printing practices of the day.

The probability is that the First Folio of 1623 had an edition of between 1,000 and 1,250 copies. It is believed that it sold for £1, which made it an expensive book, for £1 in 1623 was equivalent to something between $40 and $50 in modern purchasing power.

During the seventeenth century, Shakespeare was sufficiently popular to warrant three later editions in folio size, the Second Folio of 1632, the Third Folio of 1663–1664, and the Fourth Folio of 1685. The Third Folio added six other plays ascribed to Shakespeare, but these are apocryphal.

THE SHAKESPEAREAN THEATRE

The theatres in which Shakespeare's plays were performed were vastly different from those we know today. The stage was a platform that jutted out into the area now occupied by the first rows of seats on the main floor, which is called the "orchestra" in America and the "pit" in England. This platform had no curtain to come down at the ends of acts and scenes. And although simple stage properties were available, the Elizabethan theatre lacked both the machinery and the elaborate movable scenery of the modern theatre. In the rear of the platform stage was a curtained area that could be used as an inner room, a tomb, or any such scene that might be required. A balcony above this inner room, and perhaps balconies on the sides of the stage, could represent the upper deck of a ship, the entry to

Juliet's room, or a prison window. A trap door in the stage provided an entrance for ghosts and devils from the nether regions, and a similar trap in the canopied structure over the stage, known as the "heavens," made it possible to let down angels on a rope. These primitive stage arrangements help to account for many elements in Elizabethan plays. For example, since there was no curtain, the dramatist frequently felt the necessity of writing into his play action to clear the stage at the ends of acts and scenes. The funeral march at the end of *Hamlet* is not there merely for atmosphere; Shakespeare had to get the corpses off the stage. The lack of scenery also freed the dramatist from undue concern about the exact location of his sets, and the physical relation of his various settings to each other did not have to be worked out with the same precision as in the modern theatre.

Before London had buildings designed exclusively for theatrical entertainment, plays were given in inns and taverns. The characteristic inn of the period had an inner courtyard with rooms opening onto balconies overlooking the yard. Players could set up their temporary stages at one end of the yard and audiences could find seats on the balconies out of the weather. The poorer sort could stand or sit on the cobblestones in the yard, which was open to the sky. The first theatres followed this construction, and throughout the Elizabethan period the large public theatres had a yard in front of the stage open to the weather, with two or three tiers of covered balconies extending around the theatre. This physical structure again influenced the writing of plays. Because a dramatist wanted the actors to be heard, he frequently wrote into his play orations that could be delivered with declamatory effect. He also provided spectacle, buffoonery, and broad jests to keep the riotous groundlings in the yard entertained and quiet.

In another respect the Elizabethan theatre differed greatly from ours. It had no actresses. All women's roles were taken by boys, sometimes recruited from the boys' choirs of the London churches. Some of these youths acted their roles with great skill and the Elizabethans did not seem to be aware of any incongruity. The first actresses on the professional English stage appeared after the Restoration of Charles II, in 1660, when exiled Englishmen brought back from France practices of the French stage.

London in the Elizabethan period, as now, was the center of theatrical interest, though wandering actors from time to time traveled through the country performing in inns, halls, and the houses of the nobility. The first professional playhouse, called simply The Theatre, was erected by James Burbage, father of Shakespeare's colleague Richard Burbage, in 1576 on lands of the old Holywell Priory adjacent to Finsbury Fields, a playground and park area just north of the city walls. It had the advantage of being outside the city's jurisdiction and yet was near enough to be easily accessible. Soon after The Theatre was opened, another playhouse called The Curtain was erected in the same neighborhood. Both of these playhouses had open courtyards and were probably polygonal in shape.

About the time The Curtain opened, Richard Farrant, Master of the Children of the Chapel Royal at Windsor and of St. Paul's, conceived the idea of opening a "private" theatre in the old monastery buildings of the Blackfriars, not far from St. Paul's Cathedral in the heart of the city. This theatre was ostensibly to train the choirboys in plays for presentation at Court, but Farrant managed to present plays to paying audiences and achieved considerable success until aristocratic neighbors complained and had the theatre closed. This first Blackfriars Theatre was significant, however, because it popularized the boy actors in a professional way and it paved the way for a second theatre in the Blackfriars, which Shakespeare's company took over more than thirty years later. By the last years of the sixteenth century, London had at least six professional theatres and still others were erected during the reign of James I.

The Globe Theatre, the playhouse that most people connect with Shakespeare, was erected early in 1599 on the Bankside, the area across the Thames from the city. Its construction had a dramatic beginning, for on the night of December 28, 1598, James Burbage's sons, Cuthbert and Richard, gathered together a crew who tore down the old theatre in Holywell and carted the timbers across the river to a site that they had chosen for a new playhouse. The reason for this clandestine operation was a row with the landowner over the lease to the Holywell property. The site chosen for the Globe was another playground outside of the city's jurisdiction, a region of somewhat unsavory character. Not far away was the Bear Garden, an amphitheatre devoted to the baiting of bears and bulls. This was also the region occupied by many houses of ill fame licensed by the Bishop of Winchester and the source of substantial revenue to him. But it was easily accessible either from London Bridge or by means of the cheap boats operated by the London watermen, and it had the great advantage of being beyond the authority of the Puritanical aldermen of London, who frowned on plays because they lured apprentices from work, filled their heads with improper ideas, and generally exerted a bad influence. The aldermen also complained that the crowds drawn together in the theatre helped to spread the plague.

The Globe was the handsomest theatre up to its time. It was a large building, apparently octagonal in shape, and open like its predecessors to the sky in the center, but capable of seating a large audience in its covered balconies. To erect and operate the Globe, the Burbages organized a syndicate composed of the leading members of the dramatic company, of which Shakespeare was a member. Since it was open to the weather and depended on natural light, plays had to be given in the afternoon. This caused no hardship in the long afternoons of an English summer, but in the winter the weather was a great handicap and discouraged all except the hardiest. For that reason, in 1608 Shakespeare's company was glad to take over the lease of the second Blackfriars Theatre, a substantial, roomy hall reconstructed within the framework of the old monastery building. This theatre was protected from the weather and its stage was artificially lighted by chandeliers of candles. This became the winter play-house for Shakespeare's company and at once proved so popular that the congestion of traffic created an embarrassing problem. Stringent regulations had to be made for the movement of coaches in the vicinity. Shakespeare's company continued to use the Globe during the summer months. In 1613 a squib fired from a cannon during a performance of *Henry VIII* fell on the thatched roof and the Globe burned to the ground. The next year it was rebuilt.

London had other famous theatres. The Rose, just west of the Globe, was built by Philip Henslowe, a semiliterate denizen of the Bankside, who became one of the most important theatrical owners and producers of the Tudor and Stuart periods. What is more important for historians, he kept a detailed account book, which provides much of our information about theatrical history in his time. Another famous theatre on the Bankside was the Swan, which a Dutch priest, Johannes de Witt, visited in 1596. The crude drawing of the stage which he made was copied by his friend Arend van Buchell; it is one of the important pieces of contemporary evidence for theatrical construction. Among the other theatres, the Fortune, north of the city, on Golding Lane, and the Red Bull, even farther away from the city, off St. John's Street, were the most popular. The Red Bull, much frequented by apprentices, favored sensational and sometimes rowdy plays.

The actors who kept all of these theatres going were organized into companies under the protection of some noble patron. Traditionally actors had enjoyed a low reputation. In some of the ordinances they were classed as vagrants; in the phraseology of the time, "rogues, vagabonds, sturdy beggars, and common players" were all listed together as undesirables. To escape penalties often meted out to these characters, organized groups of actors managed to gain the protection of various personages of high degree. In the later years of Elizabeth's reign, a group flourished under the name of the Queen's Men; another group had the protection of the Lord Admiral and were known as the Lord Admiral's Men. Edward Alleyn, son-in-law of Philip Henslowe, was the leading spirit in the Lord Admiral's Men. Besides the adult companies, troupes of boy actors from time to time also enjoyed considerable popularity. Among these were the Children of Paul's and the Children of the Chapel Royal.

The company with which Shakespeare had a long association had for its first patron Henry Carey, Lord Hunsdon, the Lord Chamberlain, and hence they were known as the Lord Chamberlain's Men. After the accession of James I, they became the King's Men. This company was the great rival of the Lord Admiral's Men, managed by Henslowe and Alleyn.

All was not easy for the players in Shakespeare's time, for the aldermen of London were always eager for an excuse to close up the Blackfriars and any other theatres in their jurisdiction. The theatres outside the jurisdiction of London were not immune from interference, for they might be shut up by order of the Privy Council for meddling in politics or for various other offenses, or they might be closed in time of plague lest they spread infection. During plague times, the actors usually went on tour and played the provinces wherever they could find an audience. Particularly frightening were the plagues of 1592–1594 and 1613 when the theatres closed and the players, like many other Londoners, had to take to the country.

Though players had a low social status, they enjoyed great popularity, and one of the favorite forms of entertainment at Court was the performance of plays. To be commanded to perform at Court conferred great prestige upon a company of players, and printers frequently noted that fact when they published plays. Several of Shakespeare's plays were performed before the sovereign, and Shakespeare himself undoubtedly acted in some of these plays.

REFERENCES FOR FURTHER READING

Indispensable for anyone who wants to "study" the sonnets is the New Variorum Edition by Hyder E. Rollins (2 vols., Philadelphia, 1944). The text printed is that of the 1609 Quarto, supplemented by a sampling of editors' commentary for each sonnet from the eighteenth century onward. The second volume reprints excerpts of comment on the autobiographical question.

Several new editions of the sonnets have appeared in recent years. The edition of W. G. Ingram and Theodore Redpath (New York, 1965) devotes most of its attention to explanations of the nuances of Shakespeare's meaning in the sonnets; it also provides a detailed history of the text and an annotated list of editions. *The Sonnets, Songs, and Poems of Shakespeare,* edited by Oscar J. Campbell (New York, 1964; hard cover and paperback), has brief glossarial notes and a running commentary relating the individual sonnets to Pembroke as the friend. *Shakespeare's Sonnets,* edited by Martin Seymour-Smith (London, 1963), an old-spelling text, has excellent notes, which, however, reflect the author's certainty that the sonnets are autobiographical. He believes that the sonnets tell a discernible story indicating that a homosexual attraction, if not a physical relationship, lay behind Shakespeare's love for the friend. The edition of A. L. Rowse (New York, 1964; hard cover and paperback) presents the most recent expression of the case for Southampton as the friend. Another old-spelling text of the sonnets is printed in *A Casebook on Shakespeare's Sonnets,* edited by Gerald Willen and Victor B. Reed (paperback; New York, 1964); this volume includes a selection of interpretive essays and a nine-page bibliography of editions and critical commentary. *The Riddle of Shakespeare's Sonnets,* edited by Edward Hubler (New York, 1962), reprints the sonnets without notes, with a selection of provocative critical essays and the full text of Oscar Wilde's novelette *The Portrait of Mr. W. H.*

Such a wealth of critical comment on the sonnets exists that we list only a few recent works that are readily available. Bibliographies in the editions cited above will guide the reader to additional titles. John Dover Wilson, *An Introduction to the Sonnets of Shakespeare* (New York, 1964), reprinted as the introduction to the new Cambridge edition of the sonnets (Cambridge, Eng., 1966), contains a full discussion of the place of Shakespeare's verses in the sonnet tradition and of the autobiographical "mystery." J. W. Lever, *The Elizabethan Love Sonnet* (London, 1956) contributes valuable insights to the meaning of Shakespeare's sonnets. Also illuminating is J. B. Leishman, *Themes and Variations in Shakespeare's Sonnets* (London, 1961; paperback edition also available). Although brief, the comment by Hallett Smith, *Elizabethan Poetry: A Study in Conventions, Meaning, and Expression* (Cambridge, Mass., 1952) is a sensible introduction to the study of the sonnets. Edward Hubler, *The Sense of Shakespeare's Sonnets* (Princeton, 1952) is also stimulating. William Empson, in *Seven Types of Ambiguity* (London, 1930; rev. ed., 1947; paperback available) and *Some Versions of Pastoral* (London, 1935; paperback available), offers provocative suggestions about potential interpretations of some of the sonnets. Controversial theories as to the dating of several sonnets and autobiographical background are to be found in Leslie Hotson, *Shakespeare's Sonnets Dated, and Other Essays* (London, 1949) and *Mr. W. H.* (London, 1964).

Many readers will want suggestions for further reading about Shakespeare and his times. A few references will serve as guides to further study in the enormous literature on the subject. A simple and useful little book is Gerald Sanders, *A Shakespeare Primer* (New York, 1950). *A Companion to Shakespeare Studies,* edited by Harley Granville-Barker and G. B. Harrison (Cambridge, 1934), is a valuable guide. The most recent concise handbook of facts about Shakespeare is Gerald E. Bentley, *Shakespeare: A Biographical Handbook* (New Haven, 1961). More detailed but not so voluminous as to be confusing is Hazelton Spencer, *The Art and Life of William Shakespeare* (New York, 1940), which, like Sanders' and Bentley's handbooks, contains a brief annotated list of useful books on various aspects of the subject. The most detailed and scholarly work providing complete factual information about Shakespeare is Sir Edmund Chambers, *William Shakespeare: A Study of Facts and Problems* (2 vols., Oxford, 1930).

Among other biographies of Shakespeare, Joseph Quincy Adams, *A Life of William Shakespeare* (Boston, 1923) is still an excellent assessment of the essential facts and the traditional information, and Marchette Chute, *Shakespeare of London* (New York, 1949; paperback, 1957) stresses Shakespeare's life in the theatre. Two new biographies of Shakespeare have recently appeared. A. L. Rowse, *William Shakespeare: A Biography* (London, 1963; New York, 1964) provides an appraisal by a distinguished English historian, who dismisses the notion that somebody else wrote Shakespeare's plays as arrant nonsense that runs counter to known historical fact. Peter Quennell, *Shakespeare: A Biography* (Cleveland and New York, 1963) is a sensitive and intelligent survey of what is known and surmised of Shakespeare's life. Louis B. Wright, *Shakespeare for Everyman* (paperback; New York, 1964) discusses the basis of Shakespeare's enduring popularity.

The *Shakespeare Quarterly,* published by the Shakespeare Association of America under the editorship of James G. McManaway, is recommended for those who wish to keep up with current Shakespearean scholarship and stage productions. The *Quarterly* includes an annual bibliography of Shakespeare editions and works on Shakespeare published during the previous year.

The question of the authenticity of Shakespeare's plays arouses perennial attention. The theory of hidden cryptograms in the plays is demolished by William F. and Elizebeth S. Friedman, *The Shakespearean Ciphers Examined* (New York, 1957). A succinct account of the various absurdities advanced to suggest the authorship of a multitude of candidates other than Shakespeare will be found in R. C. Churchill, *Shakespeare and His Betters* (Bloomington, Ind., 1959). Another recent discussion of the subject, *The Authorship of Shakespeare*, by James G. McManaway (Washington, D.C., 1962), presents the evidence from contemporary records to prove the identity of Shakespeare the actor-playwright with Shakespeare of Stratford.

Scholars are not in agreement about the details of playhouse construction in the Elizabethan period. John C. Adams presents a plausible reconstruction of the Globe in *The Globe Playhouse: Its Design and Equipment* (Cambridge, Mass., 1942; 2nd rev. ed., 1961). A description with excellent drawings based on Dr. Adams' model is Irwin Smith, *Shakespeare's Globe Playhouse: A Modern Reconstruction in Text and Scale Drawings* (New York, 1956). Other sensible discussions are C. Walter Hodges, *The Globe Restored* (London, 1953) and A. M. Nagler, *Shakespeare's Stage* (New Haven, 1958). Bernard Beckerman, *Shakespeare at the Globe, 1599–1609* (New Haven, 1962; paperback, 1962) discusses Elizabethan staging and acting techniques.

A sound and readable history of the early theatres is Joseph Quincy Adams, *Shakespearean Playhouses: A History of English Theatres from the Beginnings to the Restoration* (Boston, 1917). For detailed, factual information about the Elizabethan and seventeenth-century stages, the definitive reference works are Sir Edmund Chambers, *The Elizabethan Stage* (4 vols., Oxford, 1923) and Gerald E. Bentley, *The Jacobean and Caroline Stages* (5 vols., Oxford, 1941–1956).

Further information on the history of the theatre and related topics will be found in the following titles: T. W. Baldwin, *The Organization and Personnel of the Shakespearean Company* (Princeton, 1927); Lily Bess Campbell, *Scenes and Machines on the English Stage during the Renaissance* (Cambridge, 1923); Esther Cloudman Dunn, *Shakespeare in America* (New York, 1939); George C. D. Odell, *Shakespeare from Betterton to Irving* (2 vols., London, 1931); Arthur Colby Sprague, *Shakespeare and the Actors: The Stage Business in His Plays (1660–1905)* (Cambridge, Mass., 1944) and *Shakespearian Players and Performances* (Cambridge, Mass., 1953); Leslie Hotson, *The Commonwealth and Restoration Stage* (Cambridge, Mass., 1928); Alwin Thaler, *Shakspere to Sheridan: A Book about the Theatre of Yesterday and To-day* (Cambridge, Mass., 1922); George C. Branam, *Eighteenth-Century Adaptations of Shakespeare's Tragedies* (Berkeley, 1956); C. Beecher Hogan, *Shakespeare in the*

Theatre, 1701–1800 (Oxford, 1957); Ernest Bradlee
Watson, *Sheridan to Robertson: A Study of the 19th-
Century London Stage* (Cambridge, Mass., 1926);
and Enid Welsford, *The Court Masque* (Cambridge,
Mass., 1927).

A brief account of the growth of Shakespeare's
reputation is F. E. Halliday, *The Cult of Shakespeare* (London, 1947). A more detailed discussion
is given in Augustus Ralli, *A History of Shakespearian Criticism* (2 vols., Oxford, 1932; New York,
1958). Harley Granville-Barker, *Prefaces to Shakespeare* (5 vols., London, 1927–1948; 2 vols., London,
1958) provides stimulating critical discussion of the
plays. An older classic of criticism is Andrew C.
Bradley, *Shakespearean Tragedy: Lectures on Hamlet, Othello, King Lear, Macbeth* (London, 1904;
paperback, 1955). Sir Edmund Chambers, *Shakespeare: A Survey* (London, 1935; paperback, 1958)
contains short, sensible essays on thirty-four of the
plays, originally written as introductions to single-
play editions. Alfred Harbage, *William Shakespeare:
A Reader's Guide* (New York, 1963) is a handbook
to the reading and appreciation of the plays, with
scene synopses and interpretation.

For the history plays see Lily Bess Campbell,
*Shakespeare's "Histories": Mirrors of Elizabethan
Policy* (Cambridge, 1947); John Palmer, *Political
Characters of Shakespeare* (London, 1945; 1961);
E. M. W. Tillyard, *Shakespeare's History Plays* (Lon-
don, 1948); Irving Ribner, *The English History Play
in the Age of Shakespeare* (Princeton, 1947); Max
M. Reese, *The Cease of Majesty* (London, 1961);
and Arthur Colby Sprague, *Shakespeare's Histories:*

Plays for the Stage (London, 1964). Harold Jenkins, "Shakespeare's History Plays: 1900–1951," *Shakespeare Survey 6* (Cambridge, 1953), 1-15, provides an excellent survey of recent critical opinion on the subject.

The comedies are illuminated by the following studies: C. L. Barber, *Shakespeare's Festive Comedy* (Princeton, 1959); John Russell Brown, *Shakespeare and His Comedies* (London, 1957); H. B. Charlton, *Shakespearian Comedy* (London, 1938; 4th ed., 1949); W. W. Lawrence, *Shakespeare's Problem Comedies* (New York, 1931); and Thomas M. Parrott, *Shakespearean Comedy* (New York, 1949).

Further discussions of Shakespeare's tragedies, in addition to Bradley, already cited, are contained in H. B. Charlton, *Shakespearian Tragedy* (Cambridge, 1948); Willard Farnham, *The Medieval Heritage of Elizabethan Tragedy* (Berkeley, 1936) and *Shakespeare's Tragic Frontier: The World of His Final Tragedies* (Berkeley, 1950); and Harold S. Wilson, *On the Design of Shakespearian Tragedy* (Toronto, 1957).

The "Roman" plays are treated in M. M. MacCallum, *Shakespeare's Roman Plays and Their Background* (London, 1910) and J. C. Maxwell, "Shakespeare's Roman Plays, 1900–1956," *Shakespeare Survey 10* (Cambridge, 1957), 1-11.

Kenneth Muir, *Shakespeare's Sources: Comedies and Tragedies* (London, 1957) discusses Shakespeare's use of source material. The sources themselves have been reprinted several times. Among old editions are John P. Collier (ed.), *Shakespeare's Library* (2 vols., London, 1850), Israel C. Gollancz (ed.), *The Shakespeare Classics* (12 vols., London, 1907–1926), and W. C. Hazlitt (ed.), *Shakespeare's Library* (6 vols., London, 1875). A modern edition is being prepared by Geoffrey Bullough with the title *Narrative and Dramatic Sources of Shakespeare* (London and New York, 1957–). Six volumes, covering all the plays except the tragedies, have been published to date (1967).

In addition to the second edition of *Webster's New International Dictionary*, which contains most of the unusual words used by Shakespeare, the following reference works are helpful: Edwin A. Abbott, *A Shakespearian Grammar* (London, 1872); C. T. Onions, *A Shakespeare Glossary* (2nd rev. ed., Oxford, 1925); and Eric Partridge, *Shakespeare's Bawdy* (New York, 1948; paperback, 1960).

Some knowledge of the social background of the period in which Shakespeare lived is important for a full understanding of his work. A brief, clear, and accurate account of Tudor history is S. T. Bindoff, *The Tudors*, in the Penguin series. A readable general history is G. M. Trevelyan, *The History of England*, first published in 1926 and available in numerous editions. The same author's *English Social History*, first published in 1942 and also available in many editions, provides fascinating information about England in all periods. Sir John Neale, *Queen Elizabeth* (London, 1935; paperback, 1957), is the best study of the great Queen. Various aspects of life in the Elizabethan period are treated in Louis B. Wright, *Middle-Class Culture in Elizabethan England* (Chapel Hill, N.C., 1935; reprinted Ithaca, N.Y., 1958, 1964). *Shakespeare's England: An Ac-*

count of the Life and Manners of His Age, edited by
Sidney Lee and C. T. Onions (2 vols., Oxford, 1917),
provides much information on many aspects of Elizabethan life. A fascinating survey of the period will
be found in Muriel St. C. Byrne, *Elizabethan Life
in Town and Country* (London, 1925; rev. ed., 1954;
paperback, 1961).

The Folger Library is issuing a series of illustrated
booklets entitled "Folger Booklets on Tudor and
Stuart Civilization," printed and distributed by Cornell University Press. Published to date are the
following titles:

D. W. Davies, *Dutch Influences on English Culture, 1558–1625*

Giles E. Dawson, *The Life of William Shakespeare*

Ellen C. Eyler, *Early English Gardens and Garden
Books*

Elaine W. Fowler, *English Sea Power in the Early
Tudor Period, 1485–1558*

John R. Hale, *The Art of War and Renaissance
England*

William Haller, *Elizabeth I and the Puritans*

Virginia A. LaMar, *English Dress in the Age of
Shakespeare*

———, *Travel and Roads in England*

John L. Lievsay, *The Elizabethan Image of Italy*

James G. McManaway, *The Authorship of Shakespeare*

Dorothy E. Mason, *Music in Elizabethan England*

Garrett Mattingly, *The "Invincible" Armada
and Elizabethan England*

Boies Penrose, *Tudor and Early Stuart Voyaging*

Conyers Read, *The Government of England under Elizabeth*

T. I. Rae, *Scotland in the Time of Shakespeare*

Albert J. Schmidt, *The Yeoman in Tudor and Stuart England*

Lilly C. Stone, *English Sports and Recreations*

Craig R. Thompson, *The Bible in English, 1525–1611*

———, *The English Church in the Sixteenth Century*

———, *Schools in Tudor England*

———, *Universities in Tudor England*

Louis B. Wright, *Shakespeare's Theatre and the Dramatic Tradition*

At intervals the Folger Library plans to gather these booklets in hardbound volumes. The first is *Life and Letters in Tudor and Stuart England, First Folger Series,* edited by Louis B. Wright and Virginia A. LaMar (published for the Folger Shakespeare Library by Cornell University Press, 1962). The volume contains eleven of the separate booklets.

TO THE ONLY BEGETTER OF
THESE ENSUING SONNETS
MR. W. H. ALL HAPPINESS
AND THAT ETERNITY
PROMISED
BY
OUR EVER-LIVING POET
WISHETH
THE WELL-WISHING
ADVENTURER IN
SETTING
FORTH

T.T.

SHAKESPEARE'S SONNETS

1. **increase:** offspring; fruit.

2. **beauty's rose:** i.e., beauty's finest flower.

4. **tender:** youthful; **bear his memory:** serve as a memorial of him.

5. **contracted:** betrothed.

6. **self-substantial fuel:** fuel composed of your own substance.

9. **fresh:** lovely.

10. **only:** principal; peerless; **gaudy:** delightful.

11. **content:** (1) that contained, seed; (2) happiness; i.e., take pleasure in yourself alone.

12. **churl:** (1) boor; (2) miser; **makest waste:** destroys.

14. **eat the world's due, by the grave and thee:** consume what should belong to the world by refusing to have children before you die.

⸺⸺⸺⸺⸺⸺⸺

This first sonnet urging a young man to marry strikes two themes repeated in most of the ensuing ones of the "procreation" series: that immortality is achieved by producing offspring of one's body, and that the possessor of beauty has a particular obligation to perpetuate it.

1

From fairest creatures we desire increase,
That thereby beauty's rose might never die,
But, as the riper should by time decease,   3
His tender heir might bear his memory;
But thou, contracted to thine own bright eyes,
Feedst thy light's flame with self-substantial fuel,   6
Making a famine where abundance lies,
Thyself thy foe, to thy sweet self too cruel:
Thou that art now the world's fresh ornament   9
And only herald to the gaudy spring,
Within thine own bud buriest thy content
And, tender churl, makest waste in niggarding.   12
   Pity the world, or else this glutton be,
     To eat the world's due, by the grave and thee.

"That beauty's rose might never die." From Theodor de Bry,
Emblemata nobilitati et vulgo (1592).

3. **livery:** distinguishing garb (youthful beauty).

4. **tottered:** ragged; **weed:** pun on "garment."

8. **thriftless praise:** praise that really reveals your lack of thrift; i.e., lefthanded praise.

9. **deserved thy beauty's use:** would you deserve for making profitable use of your beauty (with a pun on the sexual sense of **use.**)

11. **sum my count:** render my audit; **make my old excuse:** defend my old age from a charge of spending all the beauty entrusted to me and having nothing to show for it.

12. **by succession thine:** i.e., inherited from you.

13. **were:** would be.

〰〰〰〰〰〰〰〰〰

When age has damaged your own beauty, you will be protected against a charge of wasting your treasure if you can point to a lovely child of your own body and say that your beauty has been bequeathed to him.

2

When forty winters shall besiege thy brow
And dig deep trenches in thy beauty's field,
Thy youth's proud livery, so gazed on now,　　　3
Will be a tottered weed of small worth held:
Then being asked where all thy beauty lies,
Where all the treasure of thy lusty days,　　　6
To say within thine own deep-sunken eyes
Were an all-eating shame and thriftless praise.
How much more praise deserved thy beauty's use　　　9
If thou couldst answer, "This fair child of mine
Shall sum my count and make my old excuse,"
Proving his beauty by succession thine.　　　12
　This were to be new made when thou art old
　And see thy blood warm when thou feelst it cold.

3. **repair:** condition.

4. **beguile:** cheat; **unbless some mother:** deprive the potential mother of your child of that blessing.

5. **uneared:** unplowed.

7. **fond:** (1) foolish; (2) doting (on himself).

8. **to:** so as to; **stop posterity:** end his family line.

9. **glass:** image.

10. **Calls back:** remembers; **prime:** youth.

11. **windows of thine age:** aged eyes.

13. **rememb'red not to be:** so as not to be remembered.

||||||||||||||||||||||||||||||||||||||||

View yourself in a mirror and tell yourself that now is the time to duplicate that likeness. You are your mother's image, and it is your duty to keep that image fresh. As your mother recalls her own youth in looking at you, you could gaze at your own child and see yourself when young. But if you intend to be forgotten, die unmarried, and your image will die with you.

3

Look in thy glass, and tell the face thou viewest
Now is the time that face should form another,
Whose fresh repair if now thou not renewest,   3
Thou dost beguile the world, unbless some mother.
For where is she so fair whose uneared womb
Disdains the tillage of thy husbandry?   6
Or who is he so fond will be the tomb
Of his self-love, to stop posterity?
Thou art thy mother's glass, and she in thee   9
Calls back the lovely April of her prime;
So thou through windows of thine age shalt see,
Despite of wrinkles, this thy golden time.   12
   But if thou live rememb'red not to be,
    Die single, and thine image dies with thee.

2. **beauty's legacy:** legacy of beauty.

4. **frank . . . free:** (1) generous; (2) lusty; prodigal of body.

6. **largess:** gift.

7. **use:** (1) use up; (2) invest for profit.

8. **live:** (1) remain alive (beyond your own span of life); (2) support yourself.

9. **traffic:** business.

10. **deceive:** cheat.

14. **used:** i.e., showing profit in the form of a child.

||||||||||||||||||||||||||||||||||||

Spendthrift beauty, why do you spend all your inherited wealth of beauty on yourself? Nature does not give outright but only lends to those who are as generous as she in giving freely of themselves. Why do you use the profit of so much wealth when it will not keep you alive? for dealing only with yourself, you cheat yourself of your own continuance! How can you account to Nature for your use of her gifts under these circumstances? The remains of your beauty will be buried with you, which, if used to reproduce your line, will live in your heir.

4

Unthrifty loveliness, why dost thou spend
Upon thyself thy beauty's legacy?
Nature's bequest gives nothing but doth lend,   3
And, being frank, she lends to those are free.
Then, beauteous niggard, why dost thou abuse
The bounteous largess given thee to give?   6
Profitless usurer, why dost thou use
So great a sum of sums, yet canst not live?
For, having traffic with thyself alone,   9
Thou of thyself thy sweet self dost deceive:
Then how, when Nature calls thee to be gone,
What acceptable audit canst thou leave?   12
  Thy unused beauty must be tombed with thee,
  Which, used, lives the executor to be.

1. **gentle work:** perhaps a pun on the sense "work of gentles," the gentlefolk being his parents.

2. **gaze:** object of gaze.

4. **unfair:** make ugly; **fairly:** (1) truly; (2) in beauty.

6. **confounds:** destroys.

9. **distillation:** essence, as in a perfume.

11. **effect:** result; product (a child); **were bereft:** would be lost.

12. **Nor:** neither.

14. **Leese:** lose; **show:** appearance; **substance:** essential nature.

||||||||||||||||||||||||||||||||||||||

Time, that has gently formed you into a lovely object which all admire, will yet destroy your beauty, even as summer is destroyed by winter. But the essence of summer remains in the perfume made from its flowers.

5

Those hours that with gentle work did frame
The lovely gaze where every eye doth dwell
Will play the tyrants to the very same   3
And that unfair which fairly doth excel;
For never-resting time leads summer on
To hideous winter and confounds him there,   6
Sap checked with frost and lusty leaves quite gone,
Beauty o'ersnowed and bareness everywhere.
Then, were not summer's distillation left,   9
A liquid prisoner pent in walls of glass,
Beauty's effect with beauty were bereft,
Nor it nor no remembrance what it was: 12
  But flowers distilled, though they with winter meet,
  Leese but their show; their substance still lives
    sweet.

1. **ragged:** rough.

3. **make sweet some vial:** leave your sweet essence in some vial (womb); **treasure:** enrich.

5. **use:** profit.

6. **happies:** makes fortunate; **pay the willing loan:** willingly pay the loan.

10. **refigured thee:** copied your image.

13. **self-willed:** (1) obstinate; (2) bequeathed by yourself to yourself.

<hr>

Then do not let winter's roughening hand mar your youthful beauty before your essence has been preserved; enrich some womb with the treasure of your beauty ere you destroy yourself. Interest on a loan is not forbidden when the borrower pays it willingly in his happiness; in your case, you could breed the likeness of yourself, or—ten times happier—ten for your one. Ten copies of you would be luckier for the world than you alone; and what could Death do when you died, if you left an heir as posterity? Trust not to yourself alone; you are too lovely to be the spoil of Death and the prey of worms.

6

Then let not winter's ragged hand deface
In thee thy summer ere thou be distilled:
Make sweet some vial; treasure thou some place   3
With beauty's treasure ere it be self-killed.
That use is not forbidden usury
Which happies those that pay the willing loan;   6
That's for thyself to breed another thee,
Or ten times happier be it ten for one.
Ten times thyself were happier than thou art,   9
If ten of thine ten times refigured thee:
Then what could Death do if thou shouldst depart,
Leaving thee living in posterity?   12
  Be not self-willed, for thou art much too fair
  To be Death's conquest and make worms thine
    heir.

2. **undereye:** eye below (on earth).

3. **new-appearing:** youthful.

5. **steep-up:** steeply rising.

9. **highmost pitch:** height.

10. **reeleth from the day:** declines.

12. **tract:** path.

13. **thyself outgoing in thy noon:** living beyond the prime of your youth.

14. **get:** beget.

|||||||||||||||||||||||||||||||||

Just as the sun is gazed upon with admiration when it rises in its full strength but is ignored when it sinks, so you will be unregarded by posterity if you survive till old age without having a son.

7

Lo, in the orient when the gracious light
Lifts up his burning head, each undereye
Doth homage to his new-appearing sight,   3
Serving with looks his sacred majesty;
And, having climbed the steep-up heavenly hill,
Resembling strong youth in his middle age,   6
Yet mortal looks adore his beauty still,
Attending on his golden pilgrimage:
But when from highmost pitch, with weary car,   9
Like feeble age he reeleth from the day,
The eyes, fore duteous, now converted are
From his low tract and look another way: 12
    So thou, thyself outgoing in thy noon,
    Unlooked on diest unless thou get a son.

The car of the sun-god. From Vincenzo Cartari, *Imagini de gli dei delli antichi* (1615).

1. **Music to hear:** thou, whose voice is music; **sadly:** gravely; without delight.

4. **annoy:** hurt; i.e., why do you love what makes you sad or take pleasure in boredom.

6. **By unions married:** i.e., tuned in pairs.

7-8. **confounds/ In singleness the parts that thou shouldst bear:** figuratively, destroys by remaining single (1) the children you should have, (2) the endowments you should preserve.

10. **mutual ordering:** harmony.

14. **Thou single wilt prove none:** compare the proverb "One is no number."

Does the pairing of lute strings, with its reminder of marriage, make music displeasing to you? The harmonious tuning of the strings, which seem to produce one note, is a warning that your single performance will count for nothing.

8

Music to hear, why hearst thou music sadly?
Sweets with sweets war not, joy delights in joy:
Why lovest thou that which thou receivest not
    gladly,   3
Or else receivest with pleasure thine annoy?
If the true concord of well-tuned sounds,
By unions married, do offend thine ear,   6
They do but sweetly chide thee, who confounds
In singleness the parts that thou shouldst bear.
Mark how one string, sweet husband to another,   9
Strikes each in each by mutual ordering;
Resembling sire and child and happy mother,
Who, all in one, one pleasing note do sing;   12
   Whose speechless song, being many, seeming one,
   Sings this to thee, "Thou single wilt prove none."

3. **issueless:** childless.
4. **makeless:** mateless.
5. **still:** always.
6. **form:** image.
7. **private:** individual.
9. **Look what:** whatever.
10. **his place:** i.e., its (the expenditure's) location.
11. **beauty's waste:** the spending (destruction) of beauty.
14. **murd'rous shame:** shameful murder.

᠁᠁᠁᠁᠁᠁᠁᠁᠁᠁

Do you refuse to marry out of reluctance to leave a tearful widow when you die? But the world will mourn you, if you die childless, and your beauty will be utterly destroyed. One who can so destroy himself must be incapable of love.

9

Is it for fear to wet a widow's eye
That thou consumest thyself in single life?
Ah, if thou issueless shalt hap to die,   3
The world will wail thee like a makeless wife;
The world will be thy widow and still weep,
That thou no form of thee hast left behind,   6
When every private widow well may keep,
By children's eyes, her husband's shape in mind.
Look what an unthrift in the world doth spend   9
Shifts but his place, for still the world enjoys it;
But beauty's waste hath in the world an end,
And, kept unused, the user so destroys it: 12
   No love toward others in that bosom sits
   That on himself such murd'rous shame commits.

6. **stickst not:** do not hesitate.

7. **roof:** shelter; i.e., the family that has nurtured him.

10. **Shall hate be fairer lodged than gentle love:** is it right that you, who are so fair, should harbor hate.

11. **presence:** appearance and manner.

<hr>

Fie! how can you claim to love anyone, when you so hate yourself as to will your own destruction and that of your family? Relent and change your attitude, so that I may change my opinion; can one fairer than all others harbor hate? Be as gracious as you seem, or at least, treat yourself kindly; make another you, so that beauty's continuance is assured.

10

For shame, deny that thou bearst love to any,
Who for thyself art so unprovident:
Grant, if thou wilt, thou art beloved of many,   3
But that thou none lovest is most evident;
For thou art so possessed with murd'rous hate
That 'gainst thyself thou stickst not to conspire,   6
Seeking that beauteous roof to ruinate
Which to repair should be thy chief desire.
Oh, change thy thought, that I may change my mind;   9
Shall hate be fairer lodged than gentle love?
Be as thy presence is, gracious and kind,
Or to thyself at least kind-hearted prove: 12
   Make thee another self for love of me,
    That beauty still may live in thine or thee.

1. **thou:** i.e., your lovely image.
2. **that:** youthful beauty; **departest:** (1) parts from; (2) shares.
8. **make the world away:** end the race of mankind.
9. **store:** replenishment; i.e., procreation.
10. **featureless:** ugly.
11. **Look whom:** whomever.
12. **in bounty:** by fruitfulness.
14. **copy:** pattern.

llllllllllllllllllllllllllllllllllll

If you beget a child, your beauty will grow in him as it wanes in you. Mankind would die out in sixty years if all men refused to have children. Those like yourself, who have received Nature's greatest gift of beauty, have an obligation to reproduce it bountifully.

11

As fast as thou shalt wane, so fast thou growst
In one of thine, from that which thou departest;
And that fresh blood which youngly thou bestowst   3
Thou mayst call thine when thou from youth con-
    vertest.
Herein lives wisdom, beauty, and increase;
Without this, folly, age, and cold decay.   6
If all were minded so, the times should cease,
And threescore year would make the world away.
Let those whom Nature hath not made for store,   9
Harsh, featureless, and rude, barrenly perish:
Look whom she best endowed, she gave thee more,
Which bounteous gift thou shouldst in bounty cherish.   12
  She carved thee for her seal, and meant thereby
  Thou shouldst print more, not let that copy die.

1. **count:** note.
2. **brave:** splendid.
4. **sable:** black.
6. **erst:** formerly.
9. **question make:** speculate.
10. **among the wastes of Time must go:** i.e., will inevitably become one of the victims of Time.
14. **breed:** breeding; procreation; **brave:** defy.

⁓⁓⁓⁓⁓⁓⁓⁓⁓⁓⁓⁓⁓⁓⁓

When I consider how time passes and the seasons change, I realize that your beauty too will be destroyed. The only defense against Time's annihilation is the procreation of children.

12

When I do count the clock that tells the time
And see the brave day sunk in hideous night,
When I behold the violet past prime   3
And sable curls all silvered o'er with white,
When lofty trees I see barren of leaves,
Which erst from heat did canopy the herd,   6
And summer's green, all girded up in sheaves,
Borne on the bier with white and bristly beard:
Then of thy beauty do I question make   9
That thou among the wastes of Time must go,
Since sweets and beauties do themselves forsake
And die as fast as they see others grow;   12
    And nothing 'gainst Time's scythe can make defense
    Save breed, to brave him when he takes thee hence.

Time, the destroyer, threatening the three Graces. From Octavio
van Veen, *Emblemata Horatiana* (1684).

1. **Oh, that you were your self:** would that you had absolute control of your body and your soul.

2. **here:** on earth.

5. **hold in lease:** possess in accordance with the terms of a lease, like a piece of land.

6. **Find no determination:** come to no end, as predetermined by the lease; **were:** would be.

8. **issue:** offspring.

10. **husbandry in honor:** (1) thrifty management; (2) honorable procreation (sanctioned by marriage).

12. **barren rage:** i.e., violent action that causes barrenness.

‖‖‖‖‖‖‖‖‖‖‖‖‖‖‖‖‖‖‖‖‖‖‖‖‖‖

Would that you had eternal self-determination; but you do not, and you should take steps to prevent your destruction by creating a child that will resemble you. Only spendthrifts allow their possessions to go to waste. Follow your own father's example and beget a son.

13

Oh, that you were your self! but, love, you are
No longer yours than you yourself here live:
Against this coming end you should prepare,   3
And your sweet semblance to some other give.
So should that beauty which you hold in lease
Find no determination; then you were   6
Yourself again after yourself's decease,
When your sweet issue your sweet form should bear.
Who lets so fair a house fall to decay,   9
Which husbandry in honor might uphold
Against the stormy gusts of winter's day
And barren rage of death's eternal cold?   12
   Oh, none but unthrifts! Dear my love, you know
   You had a father; let your son say so.

2. **have astronomy:** know astrology.

6. **Pointing:** appointing; **his:** its.

8. **oft predict:** frequent omens.

10. **constant:** i.e., fixed, not wandering; **art:** knowledge.

11. **As:** elliptical for "as assures me that"; **truth and beauty shall together thrive:** (1) virtuous beauty will be perpetuated; (2) beauty will become one of the eternal verities.

12. **If from thyself to store thou wouldst convert:** if you would turn from self-absorption to breeding.

14. **doom and date:** predetermined end.

▓▓▓▓▓▓▓▓▓▓▓▓▓▓▓▓▓▓▓▓▓▓▓▓▓

I do not tell fortunes by the stars, but your beauty inspires this prediction: virtuous beauty will continue if you will turn to breeding. Otherwise, I foretell its end.

14

Not from the stars do I my judgment pluck,
And yet methinks I have astronomy;
But not to tell of good or evil luck, 3
Of plagues, of dearths, or seasons' quality;
Nor can I fortune to brief minutes tell,
Pointing to each his thunder, rain, and wind, 6
Or say with princes if it shall go well
By oft predict that I in heaven find;
But from thine eyes my knowledge I derive, 9
And, constant stars, in them I read such art
As truth and beauty shall together thrive
If from thyself to store thou wouldst convert: 12
   Or else of thee this I prognosticate,
   Thy end is Truth's and Beauty's doom and date.

2. **Holds:** continues.

4. **Whereon the stars in secret influence comment:** which the stars mysteriously influence.

7. **Vaunt:** swagger.

8. **wear their brave state out of memory:** use up their splendid youth until it is inevitably forgotten.

9. **conceit:** realization; **inconstant stay:** uncertain duration; impermanence.

11. **wasteful:** ruinous; **debateth:** contends; vies.

14. **engraft:** create you (in verse).

‖‖‖‖‖‖‖‖‖‖‖‖‖‖‖‖‖‖‖‖‖‖‖‖‖‖‖

When I regard the impermanence of life, I think of you and envision Time and inevitable decay vieing to destroy you, and I do battle with Time by recreating you in my verse.

15

When I consider everything that grows
Holds in perfection but a little moment,
That this huge stage presenteth nought but shows   3
Whereon the stars in secret influence comment;
When I perceive that men as plants increase,
Cheered and checked even by the selfsame sky,   6
Vaunt in their youthful sap, at height decrease,
And wear their brave state out of memory:
Then the conceit of this inconstant stay   9
Sets you most rich in youth before my sight,
Where wasteful Time debateth with Decay
To change your day of youth to sullied night;   12
   And, all in war with Time for love of you,
   As he takes from you, I engraft you new.

1. **wherefore:** why.
6. **unset:** unseeded.
7. **would:** would like to.
8. **counterfeit:** image.
9. **lines of life:** (1) living likenesses; (2) lineage; **repair:** restore.
10. **this time's pencil:** the brush of a contemporary artist; **pupil:** inexpert (expressing conventional humility).
12. **yourself:** i.e., exactly as you are.
13. **give away yourself:** give yourself in marriage; **keeps:** preserves; **still:** ever.
14. **And you must live drawn by your own sweet skill:** the only way you can have enduring life is to perpetuate yourself in children.

Why do you not choose a more effective method of defeating Time than by relying upon my verses to commemorate you? Now, in your prime, many virtuous women would gladly bear your children, who would more exactly resemble you than any portrait or my verbal descriptions could hope to do. Self-perpetuation in children is the only certain immortality.

16

But wherefore do not you a mightier way
Make war upon this bloody tyrant, Time?
And fortify yourself in your decay   3
With means more blessed than my barren rhyme?
Now stand you on the top of happy hours,
And many maiden gardens, yet unset,   6
With virtuous wish would bear your living flowers,
Much liker than your painted counterfeit:
So should the lines of life that life repair   9
Which this time's pencil or my pupil pen,
Neither in inward worth nor outward fair,
Can make you live yourself in eyes of men.   12
    To give away yourself keeps yourself still,
    And you must live drawn by your own sweet skill.

2. **If it were filled with your most high deserts:** if it did full justice to you.

4. **parts:** qualities; endowments.

6. **fresh numbers:** vigorous verse.

10. **old men of less truth than tongue:** proverbially, "Old men and travelers may lie by authority."

11. **true rights:** exact due; **rage:** inspirational frenzy.

12. **stretched:** strained; **antique:** ancient, and possibly also, grotesque or comic.

Even if I could depict you in my poetry as you deserve, future times would refuse to believe that any human being could be so beautiful. But your child could prove the truth of my depiction, and you would live twice, in him and in my verse.

17

Who will believe my verse in time to come
If it were filled with your most high deserts?
Though yet, heaven knows, it is but as a tomb   3
Which hides your life and shows not half your parts.
If I could write the beauty of your eyes
And in fresh numbers number all your graces,   6
The age to come would say, "This poet lies;
Such heavenly touches ne'er touched earthly faces."
So should my papers, yellowed with their age,   9
Be scorned, like old men of less truth than tongue,
And your true rights be termed a poet's rage
And stretched meter of an antique song.   12
 But were some child of yours alive that time,
 You should live twice, in it and in my rime.

4. **lease:** term; **date:** duration.
7. **fair . . . fair:** fair one . . . beauty.
8. **untrimmed:** disarrayed; made unbeautiful.
10. **owest:** possess.
12. **in eternal lines to Time thou growest:** my verse makes you as eternal as Time itself.

||||||||||||||||||||||||||||||||||

You are comparable to a summer day, but summer's beauty is brief. You, on the other hand, will enjoy eternal youth in my verse, which can make you immortal.

18

Shall I compare thee to a summer's day?
Thou art more lovely and more temperate:
Rough winds do shake the darling buds of May; 3
And summer's lease hath all too short a date.
Sometime too hot the eye of heaven shines,
And often is his gold complexion dimmed; 6
And every fair from fair sometime declines,
By chance, or Nature's changing course, untrimmed:
But thy eternal summer shall not fade, 9
Nor lose possession of that fair thou owest,
Nor shall Death brag thou wand'rest in his shade,
When in eternal lines to Time thou growest. 12
   So long as men can breathe or eyes can see,
   So long lives this, and this gives life to thee.

4. **phoenix:** a legendary bird, the phoenix, lived in a single specimen for some hundreds of years; then it made a funeral pyre and consumed itself to ashes from which arose another phoenix.

10. **antique:** (1) aging; (2) capricious.

11. **untainted:** unblemished.

﹏﹏﹏﹏﹏﹏﹏﹏﹏

All-destructive Time, do what you will to other creatures of this earth, but I forbid you to blemish my love with signs of age. Yet, even if you do your worst, my love will be eternally young in my verses.

19

Devouring Time, blunt thou the lion's paws,
And make the earth devour her own sweet brood;
Pluck the keen teeth from the fierce tiger's jaws,   3
And burn the long-lived phoenix in her blood;
Make glad and sorry seasons as thou fleetst,
And do whate'er thou wilt, swift-footed Time,   6
To the wide world and all her fading sweets,
But I forbid thee one most heinous crime:
Oh, carve not with thy hours my love's fair brow,   9
Nor draw no lines there with thine antique pen;
Him in thy course untainted do allow
For beauty's pattern to succeeding men.   12
   Yet do thy worst, old Time: despite thy wrong,
   My love shall in my verse ever live young.

Time, devouring a child. The concept of devouring Time derives
from a confusion between "Chronos" (Time) and the Greek god
Cronus, who devoured his children. From Petrarch, *Il Petrarca con
l'espositione d'Alessandro Vellutello* (1560).

1. **with Nature's own hand painted:** i.e., owing nothing to cosmetic aids.

2. **master-mistress of my passion:** i.e., master, for whom, instead of a mistress, I express my love in this poetry.

6. **Gilding:** (1) brightening; (2) enriching.

7. **hue:** form; **all hues in his controlling:** surpassing all others in appearance.

8. **amazeth:** captivates.

11. **defeated:** deprived.

13. **pricked thee out:** besides the obvious sexual allusion, (1) selected you; (2) decked you out.

14. **use:** sexual enjoyment (and possibly—with another reference to profit from investment—the child or children that may result from his love).

᛫᛫᛫᛫᛫᛫᛫᛫᛫᛫᛫᛫᛫᛫᛫᛫᛫᛫᛫᛫᛫᛫᛫᛫᛫᛫᛫

You whom I celebrate in verse have the beauty and gentle heart of a woman but lack their characteristic faithlessness. Although Nature first intended you for a woman, she gave you one thing that sealed you as a man. Since she meant you for women's sexual pleasure, then, let them enjoy it, so long as you love me.

20

A woman's face, with Nature's own hand painted,
Hast thou, the master-mistress of my passion;
A woman's gentle heart, but not acquainted   3
With shifting change, as is false women's fashion;
An eye more bright than theirs, less false in rolling,
Gilding the object whereupon it gazeth;   6
A man in hue, all hues in his controlling,
Which steals men's eyes and women's souls amazeth.
And for a woman wert thou first created,   9
Till Nature as she wrought thee fell a-doting,
And by addition me of thee defeated,
By adding one thing, to my purpose nothing.   12
    But since she pricked thee out for women's pleasure,
    Mine be thy love, and thy love's use their treasure.

1. **Muse:** i.e., poet.
2. **painted:** artificial.
3. **ornament:** (1) adornment; (2) metaphor (comparing with sun and moon, as in line 6).
4. **fair:** beauty; **rehearse:** mention in comparison.
5. **Making a couplement of proud compare:** coupling his fair one in vainglorious comparison.
7. **rare:** excellent.
8. **rondure:** globe; the earth.
13. **like of hearsay well:** like well a bit of gossip.
14. **I will not praise that purpose not to sell:** a proverbial idea; compare *Troilus and Cressida*, IV.i.80: "We'll not commend what we intend to sell."

…

I am not like poets who praise their mistresses by comparing them extravagantly with everything beautiful in heaven and earth. But if my faithful love inspires me to write truly, my love will appear as beautiful as any human being.

(Compare No. 130.)

21

So is it not with me as with that Muse
Stirred by a painted beauty to his verse,
Who heaven itself for ornament doth use,   3
And every fair with his fair doth rehearse,
Making a couplement of proud compare
With sun and moon, with earth and sea's rich gems,   6
With April's first-born flowers and all things rare
That heaven's air in this huge rondure hems.
Oh, let me, true in love, but truly write,   9
And then believe me, my love is as fair
As any mother's child, though not so bright
As those gold candles fixed in heaven's air: 12
   Let them say more that like of hearsay well;
   I will not praise that purpose not to sell.

2. **are of one date:** endure together; i.e., so long as you remain young.

4. **look I:** I expect; **my days should expiate:** i.e., must end my days.

11. **chary:** carefully.

13. **Presume not on:** do not expect.

━━━━━━━━━━━━━━━

I will not believe the signs of age I see in my face so long as you are young. Since my heart is in your body and yours in mine, I cannot be older than you. So you must be careful of yourself, as I will be of myself for your sake. And do not expect to have back your heart when I am dead; you gave me yours forever.

22

My glass shall not persuade me I am old
So long as youth and thou are of one date;
But when in thee Time's furrows I behold,   3
Then look I death my days should expiate.
For all that beauty that doth cover thee
Is but the seemly raiment of my heart,   6
Which in thy breast doth live, as thine in me:
How can I then be elder than thou art?
O, therefore, love, be of thyself so wary   9
As I, not for myself, but for thee will,
Bearing thy heart, which I will keep so chary
As tender nurse her babe from faring ill.   12
    Presume not on thy heart when mine is slain;
    Thou gavest me thine not to give back again.

1. **unperfect:** i.e., not letter perfect in his part.

2. **put besides:** put out of; made forgetful of.

3. **replete:** filled.

4. **Whose strength's abundance weakens his own heart:** i.e., the rage is so powerful that it masters the will to act. Compare *Antony and Cleopatra*, IV.xiv.59-61: "Now all labor/ Mars what it does; yea, very force entangles/ Itself with strength."

5. **for fear of trust:** fearful of being unequal to the task.

5-6. **say/ The perfect ceremony of love's rite:** express my devotion perfectly.

10. **presagers:** oracles; **speaking breast:** i.e., heart that beats loudly.

12. **that tongue:** i.e., any tongue; **more hath more expressed:** more often has spoken at greater length.

||||||||||||||||||||||||||||||||||||||

Lack of confidence and the violence of my emotion hinder the perfect expression of my love. Let my writings speak for me, then. Learn to understand the love expressed in my poetry, as the fine sensitivity of a lover should enable you to do.

23

As an unperfect actor on the stage,
Who with his fear is put besides his part,
Or some fierce thing replete with too much rage,   3
Whose strength's abundance weakens his own heart;
So I, for fear of trust, forget to say
The perfect ceremony of love's rite,   6
And in mine own love's strength seem to decay,
O'ercharged with burden of mine own love's might.
Oh, let my books be then the eloquence   9
And dumb presagers of my speaking breast,
Who plead for love, and look for recompense,
More than that tongue that more hath more expressed.   12
    Oh, learn to read what silent love hath writ:
    To hear with eyes belongs to love's fine wit.

1. **steeled:** engraved.
4. **perspective it is best painter's art:** i.e., the art of placement so that the work will be shown to best advantage (as it appears in a lover's heart) is the painter's highest art.
7. **still:** ever.
8. **his:** its; **glazed:** glassed.
13. **cunning:** skill; **want:** lack; **grace:** enhance.

<hr/>

The sight of your eyes has impressed your beauty on my heart, so that your true image must be sought for there. Our respective eyes have benefited each other: mine in drawing you truly, yours in bringing sunlight to my heart. But eyes can only describe what they see; they cannot accurately know the heart.

24

Mine eye hath played the painter and hath steeled
Thy beauty's form in table of my heart;
My body is the frame wherein 'tis held,　　　　　3
And perspective it is best painter's art.
For through the painter must you see his skill,
To find where your true image pictured lies,　　　6
Which in my bosom's shop is hanging still,
That hath his windows glazed with thine eyes.
Now see what good turns eyes for eyes have done:　9
Mine eyes have drawn thy shape, and thine for me
Are windows to my breast, wherethrough the sun
Delights to peep, to gaze therein on thee.　　　　12
　　Yet eyes this cunning want to grace their art:
　　They draw but what they see, know not the heart.

4. **Unlooked for:** unexpectedly.

6. **But:** only.

7. **in themselves:** secondary meaning: when alone and out of favor; **pride:** splendor.

9. **painful:** laborious and, perhaps, often wounded.

10. **foiled:** (1) defeated; (2) disgraced.

11. **rased:** erased.

14. **remove . . . removed:** move; change . . . forced to move or change.

‖‖‖‖‖‖‖‖‖‖‖‖‖‖‖‖‖‖‖‖‖‖‖‖‖‖‖‖

The favored of Fortune may take pride in honor and title, but I am lucky at least in that I delight in honoring you as I should. Great men's favorites and heroes are subject to change of fortune; but I am happy in sharing an affection that will be eternal.

25

Let those who are in favor with their stars
Of public honor and proud titles boast,
Whilst I, whom fortune of such triumph bars,   3
Unlooked for joy in that I honor most.
Great princes' favorites their fair leaves spread
But as the marigold at the sun's eye;   6
And in themselves their pride lies buried,
For at a frown they in their glory die.
The painful warrior famoused for fight,   9
After a thousand victories once foiled,
Is from the book of honor rased quite,
And all the rest forgot for which he toiled: 12
    Then happy I, that love and am beloved
    Where I may not remove nor be removed.

"Love's shining sun." From Octavio van Veen, *Amorum emblemata*
(1608). The verse accompanying the emblem reads:
    "As the flower heliotrope doth to the sun's course bend,
    Right so the lover doth unto his love incline;
    On her is fixed his thoughts, on her he casts his eyen,
    She is the shining sun whereto his heart doth wend."

2. **duty:** devoted service.

3. **embassage:** message; possibly the preceding group of sonnets, to which this was meant to serve as a dedication or an envoi.

4. **witness:** evidence; **wit:** ingenuity.

6. **wanting:** lacking.

7. **some good conceit:** charitable understanding.

8. **In thy soul's thought, all naked, will bestow it:** will lodge my expression of devotion, all naked as it is, in your soul.

9. **moving:** earthly existence.

10. **Points:** shines; **fair aspect:** favorable aspect in the astrological sense.

11. **tottered:** tattered.

14. **prove:** test.

▪▪▪▪▪▪▪▪▪▪▪▪▪▪▪▪▪▪▪▪▪▪▪▪▪▪▪▪▪▪▪▪

This written message is meant to show my devotion to you rather than my wit. Indeed, my devotion is such that my wit is too poor to express it fully, and I must hope that your soul will give it a charitable reception until such time as fortune improves the beggarly condition of my love.

26

Lord of my love, to whom in vassalage
Thy merit hath my duty strongly knit,
To thee I send this written embassage   3
To witness duty, not to show my wit;
Duty so great, which wit so poor as mine
May make seem bare, in wanting words to show it,   6
But that I hope some good conceit of thine
In thy soul's thought, all naked, will bestow it;
Till whatsoever star that guides my moving   9
Points on me graciously with fair aspect
And puts apparel on my tottered loving,
To show me worthy of thy sweet respect: 12
    Then may I dare to boast how I do love thee,
    Till then not show my head where thou mayst prove
        me.

1. **toil:** travel.
6. **Intend:** proceed on.
9. **imaginary sight:** ability to see in imagination.
10. **shadow:** image.
11. **ghastly:** terrifying.
12. **black:** ugly.
14. **For:** because of.

<hr />

When I go to bed exhausted, I find no rest, for my thoughts travel to you and create your image in my mind. Thus I have no rest in the day because of my body's exertions and none at night because my mind is occupied with thoughts of you.

27

Weary with toil, I haste me to my bed,
The dear repose for limbs with travel tired,
But then begins a journey in my head,   3
To work my mind when body's work's expired;
For then my thoughts, from far where I abide,
Intend a zealous pilgrimage to thee,   6
And keep my drooping eyelids open wide,
Looking on darkness which the blind do see;
Save that my soul's imaginary sight   9
Presents thy shadow to my sightless view,
Which, like a jewel hung in ghastly night,
Makes black night beauteous and her old face new.   12
   Lo, thus, by day my limbs, by night my mind,
   For thee and for myself no quiet find.

7. **to complain:** by giving me opportunity to complain.

8. **toil:** travel.

9. **please:** flatter.

10. **dost him grace:** i.e., grace him (the day) by supplying the brightness that the clouds obscure.

11. **So flatter I:** I flatter in the same way (by saying).

12. **twire:** peep; sparkle.

‖‖‖‖‖‖‖‖‖‖‖‖‖‖‖‖‖‖‖‖‖‖‖‖

Since day and night conspire to rob me of rest, I try to gain their good will by telling the day that you are bright in imitation of him and the night that you illuminate the night sky when the stars are hidden. But day continues to bring me grief, and night regularly accentuates it.

28

How can I then return in happy plight
That am debarred the benefit of rest?
When day's oppression is not eased by night,   3
But day by night and night by day oppressed,
And each, though enemies to either's reign,
Do in consent shake hands to torture me,   6
The one by toil, the other to complain
How far I toil, still farther off from thee!
I tell the day, to please him thou art bright,   9
And dost him grace when clouds do blot the heaven;
So flatter I the swart-complexioned night,
When sparkling stars twire not, thou gildst the even. 12
    But day doth daily draw my sorrows longer,
      And night doth nightly make grief's strength seem
        stronger.

1. **in disgrace:** out of favor.
3. **bootless:** unavailing.
6. **Featured:** handsome.
7. **scope:** range of talents.
8. **what I most enjoy:** my most conspicuous gifts or talents.
10. **Haply:** perhaps.
12. **sullen:** dull and dark.

▪▪▪▪▪▪▪▪▪▪▪▪▪▪▪▪▪▪▪▪▪▪▪▪▪▪▪▪▪▪▪▪▪

When I am neglected by Fortune and the world and bewail my lot, envying the endowments given to other men, I think of you and my sorrow turns to joy. Remembering your love makes me feel so richly blessed that I would not exchange my lot for a king's.

29

When, in disgrace with Fortune and men's eyes,
I all alone beweep my outcast state,
And trouble deaf heaven with my bootless cries,   3
And look upon myself and curse my fate,
Wishing me like to one more rich in hope,
Featured like him, like him with friends possessed,   6
Desiring this man's art and that man's scope,
With what I most enjoy contented least;
Yet in these thoughts myself almost despising,   9
Haply I think on thee, and then my state,
Like to the lark at break of day arising
From sullen earth, sings hymns at heaven's gate;   12
  For thy sweet love rememb'red such wealth brings
  That then I scorn to change my state with kings.

1. **sessions:** sittings or hearings, as of a court.
4. **with old woes new wail my dear time's waste:** while newly lamenting old woes also wail the loss of my best time (youth).
6. **dateless:** interminable; endless.
8. **expense:** loss.
10. **heavily:** mournfully; **tell:** count.

<hr />

When I remember past sorrows and dear friends dead and gone, I grieve as deeply as though I had not already done so. But if I think of you, both loss and sorrow vanish.

30

When to the sessions of sweet silent thought
I summon up remembrance of things past,
I sigh the lack of many a thing I sought,   3
And with old woes new wail my dear time's waste:
Then can I drown an eye, unused to flow,
For precious friends hid in death's dateless night,   6
And weep afresh love's long since cancelled woe,
And moan the expense of many a vanished sight.
Then can I grieve at grievances foregone,   9
And heavily from woe to woe tell o'er
The sad account of fore-bemoaned moan,
Which I new pay as if not paid before.   12
    But if the while I think on thee, dear friend,
    All losses are restored and sorrows end.

1. **endeared with:** made more precious by possession of.
2. **lacking:** missing.
3. **parts:** qualities.
5. **obsequious:** appropriate to funeral rites.
6. **dear religious love:** sincere and faithful devotion.
7. **interest:** legal due.
8. **removed:** absent.
10. **trophies:** memorials; **lovers:** dear friends.
11. **parts of:** shares in.
12. **due:** right.
13. **Their images I loved:** the images of those I loved.
14. **all they:** uniting in yourself all I loved in them.

||||||||||||||||||||||||||||||||

You are the more precious to me as embodying all the friends I have loved. In you I see them all, which makes me wholly yours.

31

Thy bosom is endeared with all hearts,
Which I by lacking have supposed dead;
And there reigns love, and all love's loving parts,　　　3
And all those friends which I thought buried.
How many a holy and obsequious tear
Hath dear religious love stol'n from mine eye,　　　6
As interest of the dead, which now appear
But things removed that hidden in thee lie!
Thou art the grave where buried love doth live,　　　9
Hung with the trophies of my lovers gone,
Who all their parts of me to thee did give,
That due of many now is thine alone.　　　12
　　Their images I loved I view in thee,
　　And thou, all they, hast all the all of me.

1. **my well-contented day:** day when I shall be content (to welcome Death).
2. **churl:** boor.
3. **by fortune:** perhaps.
5. **the bett'ring of the time:** i.e., the better poetry of another age.
7. **Reserve:** keep.
8. **happier:** more talented.
10. **Muse:** inspiration.
12. **equipage:** furnishing; dress.

‖‖‖‖‖‖‖‖‖‖‖‖‖‖‖‖‖‖‖‖‖‖‖‖‖‖‖‖

If you outlive me and sometime happen to reread these verses from your dead friend, do not scorn them because they cannot measure up to the improved poetry of a new age: read the new poetry for its style; but read mine for the love expressed therein.

32

If thou survive my well-contented day
When that churl Death my bones with dust shall
    cover,
And shalt by fortune once more resurvey   3
These poor rude lines of thy deceased lover,
Compare them with the bett'ring of the time,
And though they be outstripped by every pen,   6
Reserve them for my love, not for their rhyme,
Exceeded by the height of happier men.
Oh, then vouchsafe me but this loving thought: 9
"Had my friend's Muse grown with this growing age,
A dearer birth than this his love had brought
To march in ranks of better equipage;   12
    But since he died, and poets better prove,
      Theirs for their style I'll read, his for his love."

2. **Flatter:** enhance; **sovereign:** royal.
5. **Anon:** before long; **basest:** lowest.
6. **rack:** drift.
8. **disgrace:** disfigurement.
11. **out alack:** alas.
12. **region cloud:** cloud of the lowest region of the air.
14. **stain:** (1) dim; be obscured; (2) withdraw favor.

━━━━━━━━━━━━━━━━

I have often seen the sun transform the scene with its golden rays and soon allow itself to be dimmed by low cloud. In the same way, the sun of my love's favor briefly glorified me and is now withdrawn. Yet I do not love him less for this: mortal suns may withdraw their favor, since even the heavenly sun does so.

33

Full many a glorious morning have I seen
Flatter the mountaintops with sovereign eye,
Kissing with golden face the meadows green,   3
Gilding pale streams with heavenly alchemy;
Anon permit the basest clouds to ride
With ugly rack on his celestial face,   6
And from the forlorn world his visage hide,
Stealing unseen to west with this disgrace:
Even so my sun one early morn did shine   9
With all-triumphant splendor on my brow;
But, out alack, he was but one hour mine;
The region cloud hath masked him from me now.   12
   Yet him for this my love no whit disdaineth;
   Suns of the world may stain, when heaven's sun
      staineth.

4. **brav'ry:** splendor (as the sun); **rotten:** infectious.
8. **disgrace:** scar.
9. **physic:** medicine.
13. **sheeds:** sheds.
14. **ransom:** redeem; pay for.

Why did you deceive me with false promise of continued favor, so that I was taken unawares by the cloud that has come between us? Smiling again upon me cannot make up for my humiliation, nor can your repentance give me back the trust I have lost. But your loving tears are so precious that I cannot but forgive you.

34

Why didst thou promise such a beauteous day
And make me travel forth without my cloak,
To let base clouds o'ertake me in my way,　　　　3
Hiding thy brav'ry in their rotten smoke?
'Tis not enough that through the cloud thou break,
To dry the rain on my storm-beaten face,　　　　6
For no man well of such a salve can speak
That heals the wound and cures not the disgrace.
Nor can thy shame give physic to my grief;　　　　9
Though thou repent, yet I have still the loss;
The offender's sorrow lends but weak relief
To him that bears the strong offense's cross.　　　　12
　　Ah, but those tears are pearl which thy love sheeds,
　　And they are rich and ransom all ill deeds.

3. **stain:** (1) darken; (2) blemish.

4. **canker:** cankerworm.

5. **make faults:** commit offenses.

6. **with compare:** by comparisons.

7. **corrupting:** infecting; **salving thy amiss:** (1) smoothing over your trespass; (2) healing your disease.

8. **Excusing thy sins more than thy sins are:** i.e., offering you more forgiveness for your sins than they need.

9. **sense:** reason.

13. **accessary:** old form of "accessory"; accomplice.

14. **sourly:** with bitter (cruel) effect.

||||||||||||||||||||||||||||||||||

Cease grieving for your fault. Nothing and no one is without flaw, and I myself will argue in your defense. Torn as I am between love and hate, I am both your victim and your accomplice.

35

No more be grieved at that which thou hast done:
Roses have thorns, and silver fountains mud;
Clouds and eclipses stain both moon and sun,   3
And loathsome canker lives in sweetest bud.
All men make faults, and even I in this,
Authorizing thy trespass with compare,   6
Myself corrupting, salving thy amiss,
Excusing thy sins more than thy sins are:
For to thy sensual fault I bring in sense   9
(Thy adverse party is thy advocate)
And 'gainst myself a lawful plea commence;
Such civil war is in my love and hate   12
   That I an accessary needs must be
   To that sweet thief which sourly robs from me.

5. **one respect:** one object of regard (each other).

6. **separable spite:** spiteful separation.

7. **sole:** (1) unique; (2) single.

9. **evermore:** ever again; **acknowledge:** show familiarity with.

14. **As:** that; **mine is thy good report:** your reputation is as dear as my own. The same couplet ends No. 96.

<hr />

Although our mutual love makes us as one person, we must part, lest you become dishonored by association with me. My love for you is such that I feel your reputation is in my keeping.

36

Let me confess that we two must be twain,
Although our undivided loves are one:
So shall those blots that do with me remain,   3
Without thy help by me be borne alone.
In our two loves there is but one respect,
Though in our lives a separable spite,   6
Which though it alter not love's sole effect,
Yet doth it steal sweet hours from love's delight.
I may not evermore acknowledge thee,   9
Lest my bewailed guilt should do thee shame;
Nor thou with public kindness honor me
Unless thou take that honor from thy name.   12
  But do not so: I love thee in such sort
  As, thou being mine, mine is thy good report.

"Union is love's wish." From Octavio van Veen, *Amorum emblemata* (1608). The accompanying verse reads:
  "The lover's long desire his hope doth keep contented,
  That lastly with his love united he agree.
  One mind in bodies twain may well conjoined be,
  But yet with pain to both when bodies are absented."

3. **made lame by Fortune's dearest spite:** i.e., not literally lame, although commentators have speculated on the point, but handicapped, perhaps referring to being of humbler birth than his friend. **Dearest** means "most grievous."

4. **of:** in; **truth:** honor.

7. **Entitled in thy parts, do crowned sit:** may rightly claim predominance among your qualities.

8. **make my love engrafted to this store:** attach my love to this abundance, upon which it feeds.

10. **shadow:** conception (in the poet's mind).

12. **by a part of all thy glory live:** i.e., subsist on my love for you, which I have grafted to your glorious qualities.

13. **Look what:** whatever.

||||||||||||||||||||||||||||||||||||||||

Spited by Fortune as I am, I take consolation in the many endowments you have received. To the gifts you already possess, I add my love and no longer am unlucky, because I share vicariously in your good fortune. I wish you whatever is best in the world and, having this wish, am ten times blessed myself!

37

As a decrepit father takes delight
To see his active child do deeds of youth,
So I, made lame by Fortune's dearest spite,   3
Take all my comfort of thy worth and truth.
For whether beauty, birth, or wealth, or wit,
Or any of these all, or all, or more,   6
Entitled in thy parts, do crowned sit,
I make my love engrafted to this store.
So then I am not lame, poor, nor despised,   9
Whilst that this shadow doth such substance give,
That I in thy abundance am sufficed
And by a part of all thy glory live.   12
    Look what is best, that best I wish in thee:
    This wish I have; then ten times happy me!

"Like fortune to both." From Octavio van Veen, *Amorum emblemata* (1608). The verse reads:
    "Fortune one cup doth fill equal to lovers twain;
    And howsoe'er the taste be either sour or sweet,
    To one and unto both it equally is meet,
    That either have his part in pleasure or in pain."

1. **want subject to invent:** lack an inspiring theme.
3. **argument:** theme.
4. **vulgar:** common; **rehearse:** recite.
5. **in me:** of mine.
6. **stand against thy sight:** comes to your eyes.
12. **numbers:** rhymes; **date:** duration.
13. **curious:** hypercritical; fastidious.
14. **pain:** trouble.

<hr />

I cannot be at a loss for subject matter so long as you live. The most uninspired poet could write of you. Consent to be the tenth Muse, ten times more powerful than the Nine Muses the poets invoke. And let the poet who invokes your name write immortal poetry. If my weak inventions please these critical days, the praise is rightfully yours.

38

How can my Muse want subject to invent
While thou dost breathe, that pourst into my verse
Thine own sweet argument, too excellent   3
For every vulgar paper to rehearse?
Oh, give thyself the thanks if aught in me
Worthy perusal stand against thy sight,   6
For who's so dumb that cannot write to thee,
When thou thyself dost give invention light?
Be thou the tenth Muse, ten times more in worth   9
Than those old nine which rhymers invocate;
And he that calls on thee, let him bring forth
Eternal numbers to outlive long date.   12
    If my slight Muse do please these curious days,
    The pain be mine, but thine shall be the praise.

1. **manners:** decorum.

5. **Even for this:** for this reason, if for no other.

12. **time and thoughts:** i.e., a melancholy time; **deceive:** beguile.

13. **to make one twain:** i.e., to make two persons out of one, by creating you here in imagination, while your body is elsewhere.

||||||||||||||||||||||||||||||||||||||

How can I modestly praise you, who contain the better part of myself? Let us separate, so that I may give you the credit you deserve and none will cling to me because of our association in the world's mind. Even absence from you will have the compensation that solitude will permit me time to think of our love and bring you to me in imagination.

39

Oh, how thy worth with manners may I sing,
When thou art all the better part of me?
What can mine own praise to mine own self bring,　　3
And what is't but mine own when I praise thee?
Even for this let us divided live
And our dear love lose name of single one,　　6
That by this separation I may give
That due to thee which thou deservest alone.
O absence, what a torment wouldst thou prove,　　9
Were it not thy sour leisure gave sweet leave
To entertain the time with thoughts of love,
Which time and thoughts so sweetly doth deceive,　　12
　　And that thou teachest how to make one twain
　　By praising him here who doth hence remain!

"Contentment in conceit." From Octavio van Veen, *Amorum emblemata* (1608). The verse reads:
　　"Love's recompense is oft but ev'n the thoughts of love,
　　Imagining he sees his mistress' lovely face;
　　And though she absent be, he thinks she is in place,
　　And thus this all he hath nothing at all doth prove."

5. **for my love:** because of your love for me; **my love receivest:** enjoy my mistress.

6. **for:** because; **usest:** employ in a sexual sense, as in No. 2.

7. **this self:** myself.

8. **willful:** wanton; lustful; **what thy self refusest:** what your better self rejects; i.e., the lust provoked by such a woman.

10. **all my poverty:** the little I have.

12. **love's wrong:** wrong done by a lover; **hate's known injury:** the injury of an enemy, which is expected.

13. **Lascivious:** (1) lewd; (2) wicked.

‖‖‖‖‖‖‖‖‖‖‖‖‖‖‖‖‖‖‖‖‖‖‖‖‖‖‖

If you take all my loves, you gain nothing that you had not already, for all my true love belongs to you. If you approve my mistress, I cannot complain, so long as you love her for my sake. But you merit blame if you go against your better self in indulging lust. The wrong of the friend I love is more painful than an enemy's malice. But your charm surpasses even your graceless behavior; no matter how you hurt me, we must not be enemies.

40

Take all my loves, my love, yea, take them all:
What hast thou then more than thou hadst before?
No love, my love, that thou mayst true love call: 3
All mine was thine before thou hadst this more.
Then, if for my love thou my love receivest,
I cannot blame thee for my love thou usest;   6
But yet be blamed if thou this self deceivest
By willful taste of what thy self refusest.
I do forgive thy robb'ry, gentle thief,   9
Although thou steal thee all my poverty;
And yet love knows it is a greater grief
To bear love's wrong than hate's known injury.   12
    Lascivious grace, in whom all ill well shows,
    Kill me with spites, yet we must not be foes.

1. **pretty:** charming (with ironic intent); **liberty:** (1) freedom; (2) licentiousness.

4. **still:** ever.

5. **Gentle:** secondary sense: gently born; **to be won:** i.e., because you will not woo yourself and are worth winning.

9. **my seat forbear:** leave my property (mistress) alone.

11. **riot:** unrestrained revel.

▬▬▬▬▬▬▬▬▬▬▬▬▬

It is only natural that a handsome youth like yourself should sometimes have a fling with women, since they will inevitably pursue you. But you should at least resist the youthful temptation to trifle with my mistress, since both of you thus break your faith with me.

41

Those pretty wrongs that liberty commits,
When I am sometime absent from thy heart,
Thy beauty and thy years full well befits,   3
For still temptation follows where thou art.
Gentle thou art, and therefore to be won;
Beauteous thou art, therefore to be assailed;   6
And when a woman woos, what woman's son
Will sourly leave her till she have prevailed?
Ay me, but yet thou mightst my seat forbear,   9
And chide thy beauty and thy straying youth,
Who lead thee in their riot even there
Where thou art forced to break a twofold truth: 12
    Hers, by thy beauty tempting her to thee,
    Thine, by thy beauty being false to me.

3. **is of my wailing chief:** is the main cause of my sorrow.

4. **nearly:** deeply.

7. **abuse:** betray.

8. **Suff'ring:** permitting; **approve:** prove, in the sense "try."

9. **love's:** mistress'.

14. **flattery:** gratifying delusion.

‖‖‖‖‖‖‖‖‖‖‖‖‖‖‖‖‖‖‖‖‖‖‖‖‖

I do not sorrow solely because you have stolen my mistress but more because she has estranged you from me. I can excuse you both on the grounds that you love each other for my sake, and you and my mistress possess in each other the love that I have lost. This consolation remains to me: you and I are one, so, in loving you, my mistress loves only me.

42

That thou hast her, it is not all my grief,
And yet it may be said I loved her dearly:
That she hath thee is of my wailing chief,   3
A loss in love that touches me more nearly.
Loving offenders, thus I will excuse ye:
Thou dost love her because thou knowst I love her,   6
And for my sake even so doth she abuse me,
Suff'ring my friend for my sake to approve her.
If I lose thee, my loss is my love's gain;   9
And, losing her, my friend hath found that loss:
Both find each other, and I lose both twain,
And both for my sake lay on me this cross.   12
   But here's the joy: my friend and I are one;
   Sweet flattery! then she loves but me alone.

1. **wink:** close my eyes.

2. **unrespected:** secondary meaning: "unrespectively" (without attention).

4. **darkly bright:** mysteriously lit behind the lids that darken them; **bright in dark directed:** directed toward brightness (the image of you) in the dark.

5. **shadow:** image.

6. **shadow's form:** reality; **form happy show:** appear a lovely form.

11. **imperfect:** i.e., unreal.

12. **stay:** secondary sense: comfort.

13. **to see:** so far as seeing goes.

14. **thee me:** thee to me.

||||||||||||||||||||||||||||||||||||

My eyes see more clearly at night, for then your image appears to me in dreams more vividly than anything I look upon in daylight. If your mere image has such brilliance, how much more striking must be the reality! Days are dark without the sight of you, and nights are bright as day when you appear to me in dreams.

(Compare No. 27.)

43

When most I wink, then do mine eyes best see,
For all the day they view things unrespected;
But when I sleep, in dreams they look on thee   3
And, darkly bright, are bright in dark directed.
Then thou, whose shadow shadows doth make bright,
How would thy shadow's form, form happy show   6
To the clear day with thy much clearer light
When to unseeing eyes thy shade shines so!
How would, I say, mine eyes be blessed made   9
By looking on thee in the living day,
When in dead night thy fair imperfect shade
Through heavy sleep on sightless eyes doth stay!   12
   All days are nights to see till I see thee,
    And nights bright days when dreams do show thee
    me.

1. **dull:** heavy.
2. **Injurious:** unjust.
4. **where:** to where.
8. **he:** i.e., thought.
9. **thought . . . thought:** melancholy . . . imagination.
11. **earth and water:** two of the chief elements of the human body, according to contemporary belief.
12. **attend Time's leisure:** i.e., wait until Time condescends to allow our meeting.
13. **elements:** earth and water.
14. **badges of either's woe:** i.e., symbols of grief appropriate to earth and water, with a secondary meaning for **either's:** each other's (your and my).

If my heavy flesh were as light as thought, I could be by your side with instant speed. But I realize with sorrow that I am composed of earth and water, whose heaviness weights me down and brings me only tears symbolic of their qualities.

44

If the dull substance of my flesh were thought,
Injurious distance should not stop my way;
For then, despite of space, I would be brought,   3
From limits far remote, where thou dost stay.
No matter then although my foot did stand
Upon the farthest earth removed from thee;   6
For nimble thought can jump both sea and land
As soon as think the place where he would be.
But, ah, thought kills me that I am not thought,   9
To leap large lengths of miles when thou art gone,
But that, so much of earth and water wrought,
I must attend Time's leisure with my moan,   12
    Receiving naught by elements so slow
    But heavy tears, badges of either's woe.

1. **two:** i.e., of the four elements, two of which are named in the preceding sonnet; **slight:** light; **purging:** purifying.

5. **quicker:** livelier.

8. **melancholy:** the humor **melancholy,** according to contemporary theory, corresponded to the element earth in being cold and dry.

9. **recured:** restored.

11. **even but now:** i.e., just as the poet sinks under the weight of melancholy.

14. **straight:** immediately; **sad:** heavy with sorrow.

▬▬▬▬▬▬▬▬▬▬▬▬

Wherever I am, my vital spirits constantly fly to you and leave me heavy with melancholy. When they return, I am briefly revitalized, until they fly off to you again.

45

The other two, slight air and purging fire,
Are both with thee, wherever I abide;
The first my thought, the other my desire,　　　　3
These present-absent with swift motion slide.
For when these quicker elements are gone
In tender embassy of love to thee,　　　　6
My life, being made of four, with two alone
Sinks down to death, oppressed with melancholy;
Until life's composition be recured　　　　9
By those swift messengers returned from thee,
Who even but now come back again, assured
Of thy fair health, recounting it to me.　　　　12
　　This told, I joy; but then, no longer glad,
　　I send them back again and straight grow sad.

2. **thy sight:** the sight of you.

3. **Mine eye my heart thy picture's sight would bar:** my eye would debar my heart from the sight of your picture.

4. **My heart mine eye the freedom of that right:** my heart would deny my eye that exclusive right.

5. **thou in him dost lie:** he possesses your true self.

6. **closet:** private receptacle or chamber; **crystal:** i.e., transparent and fragile, hence capable of only superficial sight, not of seeing into the heart.

9. **'cide:** decide; **title:** legal right.

10. **quest:** jury; **tenants to the heart:** partial, therefore, to the heart's side.

12. **moiety:** share.

13. **outward part:** external appearance.

||||||||||||||||||||||||||||||||||||||||

My heart and eye debate as to which sees you more truly. The verdict rendered by my thoughts, which my heart controls, is that my eye's function is to regard your person and my heart's to contemplate your love.

(Compare No. 24.)

46

Mine eye and heart are at a mortal war
How to divide the conquest of thy sight;
Mine eye my heart thy picture's sight would bar,	3
My heart mine eye the freedom of that righ'
My heart doth plead that thou in him dost lie—
A closet never pierced with crystal eyes—	6
But the defendant doth that plea deny
And says in him thy fair appearance lies.
To 'cide this title is impanelled	9
A quest of thoughts, all tenants to the heart,
And by their verdict is determined
The clear eye's moiety and the dear heart's part:	12
    As thus: mine eye's due is thy outward part,
    And my heart's right thy inward love of heart.

1. **league is took:** pact is made.
3. **When that:** when.
4. **heart in love:** lovestruck heart.
10. **still:** continually.

<hr/>

My eye and heart have become allies. When my eye is starved for the sight of you or my heart pines for you in absence, my eye feasts on your picture and invites my heart to join it. Another time, my heart invites my eye to partake of its loving thoughts. Though absent, you are ever with me, through the medium either of your picture or of my thoughts.

47

Betwixt mine eye and heart a league is took,
And each doth good turns now unto the other:
When that mine eye is famished for a look,   3
Or heart in love with sighs himself doth smother,
With my love's picture then my eye doth feast
And to the painted banquet bids my heart;   6
Another time mine eye is my heart's guest
And in his thoughts of love doth share a part.
So, either by thy picture or my love,   9
Thyself away are present still with me;
For thou not farther than my thoughts canst move,
And I am still with them and they with thee;   12
  Or, if they sleep, thy picture in my sight
  Awakes my heart to heart's and eye's delight.

1. **took my way:** set out to travel.
2. **truest:** safest.
3. **to:** for.
4. **sure wards of trust:** absolutely trustworthy keeping; certain protection.
5. **to whom:** in comparison with whom; **jewels:** not necessarily to be taken as indicating that Shakespeare had valuable jewels, probably meaning "valuables" in a more general sense.
6. **comfort:** delight; **grief:** i.e., because absent.
7. **only care:** dearest object of concern.
12. **part:** depart.
14. **truth:** honesty itself.

‖‖‖‖‖‖‖‖‖‖‖‖‖‖‖‖‖‖‖‖‖‖‖‖‖‖‖‖

When I set out on a journey, I cautiously lock up all my valuables, which are trifles compared with my regard for you. But I cannot protect myself against those who would steal you, for you are a prize that would tempt honesty itself.

48

How careful was I, when I took my way,
Each trifle under truest bars to thrust,
That to my use it might unused stay,   3
From hands of falsehood, in sure wards of trust!
But thou, to whom my jewels trifles are,
Most worthy comfort, now my greatest grief,   6
Thou best of dearest, and mine only care,
Art left the prey of every vulgar thief.
Thee have I not locked up in any chest,   9
Save where thou art not, though I feel thou art,
Within the gentle closure of my breast,
From whence at pleasure thou mayst come and part;   12
    And even thence thou wilt be stol'n, I fear,
    For truth proves thievish for a prize so dear.

1. **Against that time:** in preparation for that time.

3. **Whenas:** when; **cast his utmost sum:** made its final reckoning (and closed the book).

4. **advised respects:** prudent considerations.

5. **strangely:** with a stranger's aloofness.

7. **converted:** transformed.

8. **of settled gravity:** for staid decorum.

9. **ensconce me:** shelter myself.

10. **desert:** simply "merit," with no definite implication of worthiness.

11. **my hand against myself uprear:** raise my hand against myself, as though taking an oath as a witness, by writing this.

12. **guard:** defend.

14. **why to love:** why you should love me.

‖‖‖‖‖‖‖‖‖‖‖‖‖‖‖‖‖‖‖‖‖‖‖‖‖‖

In anticipation of the day when you shall cease to love me and begin to dwell on my faults, when you shall pass me without a greeting, when it seems prudent to give me up—in anticipation of that time—I forestall attack by self-evaluation and use my own hand to write these lines sanctioning your rightful act. It is lawful for you to leave me, since there is no reason why you should love me.

(Compare No. 88.)

49

Against that time, if ever that time come,
When I shall see thee frown on my defects,
Whenas thy love hath cast his utmost sum,   3
Called to that audit by advised respects;
Against that time when thou shalt strangely pass
And scarcely greet me with that sun thine eye,   6
When love, converted from the thing it was,
Shall reasons find of settled gravity:
Against that time do I ensconce me here   9
Within the knowledge of mine own desert,
And this my hand against myself uprear
To guard the lawful reasons on thy part.   12
  To leave poor me thou hast the strength of laws,
  Since why to love I can allege no cause.

1. **heavy:** sorrowfully.
3. **Doth teach that ease and that repose to say:** i.e., forces me even in my moments of rest to recite the painful thought.
6. **dully:** slowly; **to bear that weight:** because of bearing the weight of my woe as well as my physical weight.
8. **speed, being made:** making speed.

Travel from your side is sorrowful and slow; and rest at the end of the weary day's travel only gives me time to realize how far away from you I am. My spurs cannot drive the horse that bears me any faster but only provoke groans, which remind me that grief lies ahead.

50

How heavy do I journey on the way,
When what I seek (my weary travel's end)
Doth teach that ease and that repose to say, 3
"Thus far the miles are measured from thy friend."
The beast that bears me, tired with my woe,
Plods dully on, to bear that weight in me, 6
As if by some instinct the wretch did know
His rider loved not speed, being made from thee.
The bloody spur cannot provoke him on 9
That sometimes anger thrusts into his hide,
Which heavily he answers with a groan,
More sharp to me than spurring to his side; 12
  For that same groan doth put this in my mind:
  My grief lies onward and my joy behind.

1. **slow offense:** fault of slowness.
4. **posting:** riding with all speed.
6. **swift extremity:** utmost swiftness.
11. **neigh, no dull flesh in his fiery race:** desire is compared to a horse that neighs with impatience; but, unlike the actual horse, desire includes the element of fire but not earth.
12. **love, for love:** charity, in exchange for the sympathy shown by the horse in going slowly; **jade:** nag.
14. **go:** walk.

▪▪▪▪▪▪▪▪▪▪▪▪▪▪▪▪▪▪▪▪▪▪▪▪▪▪▪▪▪▪

Thus my love excuses the slowness of my horse, going from you. But how can the beast justify slowness when I go toward you? Then the utmost speed will not content me and no horse can go fast enough. Still, for the sake of his sympathetic slowness in my outward journey, I forgive the poor animal and allow him to walk while my spirit races ahead.

51

Thus can my love excuse the slow offense
Of my dull bearer when from thee I speed:
From where thou art why should I haste me thence? 3
Till I return, of posting is no need.
Oh, what excuse will my poor beast then find,
When swift extremity can seem but slow? 6
Then should I spur, though mounted on the wind,
In winged speed no motion shall I know.
Then can no horse with my desire keep pace; 9
Therefore desire, of perfectst love being made,
Shall neigh, no dull flesh in his fiery race;
But love, for love, thus shall excuse my jade: 12
　　Since from thee going he went willful slow,
　　Toward thee I'll run and give him leave to go.

1. **So am I:** I am exactly like; **rich:** rich man.
4. **For:** for fear of; **seldom:** infrequent.
5. **solemn:** ceremonious.
8. **captain:** chief, principal; **carcanèt:** necklace.
9. **keeps you:** (1) keeps you from me; (2) safeguards you; **as:** like.
12. **his:** its; **pride:** splendor.
13. **gives scope:** makes one free; enables one.
14. **triumph:** delight.

||||||||||||||||||||||||||||||||||||

I am like the rich man who keeps his greatest treasures locked up and looks upon them rarely so that his pleasure in them will not be spoiled by familiarity. Similarly, our meetings are made all the more delightful by their rareness. So great are your qualities that your presence delights, while your absence occasions hopeful expectation of reunion.

52

So am I as the rich, whose blessed key
Can bring him to his sweet up-locked treasure,
The which he will not ev'ry hour survey,   3
For blunting the fine point of seldom pleasure.
Therefore are feasts so solemn and so rare,
Since, seldom coming, in the long year set,   6
Like stones of worth they thinly placed are,
Or captain jewels in the carcanet.
So is the time that keeps you as my chest,   9
Or as the wardrobe which the robe doth hide,
To make some special instant special blest
By new unfolding his imprisoned pride.   12
   Blessed are you, whose worthiness gives scope,
   Being had, to triumph, being lacked, to hope.

2. **shadows:** images; **tend:** attend, in the sense to wait upon.

3. **shade:** shadow.

4. **but one:** only one person; **shadow lend:** image supply.

5. **counterfeit:** picture.

7. **On Helen's cheek all art of beauty set:** describe Helen of Troy as the acme of beauty.

8. **tires:** attires.

9. **spring:** the season, with all its fresh loveliness; **foison:** "the teeming autumn" of sonnet 97.

∎∎∎∎∎∎∎∎∎∎∎∎∎∎∎∎∎∎∎∎∎∎∎∎∎∎∎

What are you made of, that you can embody innumerable images? Both Adonis and Helen are inferior to you in beauty. In you are both the loveliness of spring and the rich abundance of autumn. Everything that appears beautiful resembles you, but you surpass everyone in fidelity of heart.

53

What is your substance, whereof are you made,
That millions of strange shadows on you tend?
Since every one hath, every one, one shade,   3
And you, but one, can every shadow lend.
Describe Adonis, and the counterfeit
Is poorly imitated after you.   6
On Helen's cheek all art of beauty set,
And you in Grecian tires are painted new.
Speak of the spring and foison of the year: 9
The one doth shadow of your beauty show,
The other as your bounty doth appear,
And you in every blessed shape we know.   12
　　In all external grace you have some part,
　　But you like none, none you, for constant heart.

2. **By:** because of; **truth:** constancy; unchangeable veracity.

5. **canker blooms:** dog roses, which have little scent.

6. **tincture:** color.

9. **for:** because; **show:** appearance; i.e., they have no perfume.

10. **unrespected:** unregarded.

11. **to themselves:** (1) by themselves; (2) singly, without consequence.

13. **lovely:** lovable.

‖‖‖‖‖‖‖‖‖‖‖‖‖‖‖‖‖‖‖‖‖‖‖‖

Constancy is a great adornment of beauty. Roses are the more admired for their scent, and although the scentless wild rose may be as colorful as the cultivated kind, its beauty ends with its death. Scented roses, however, are distilled into lasting perfume. When your youth and beauty are gone, the essence of your virtue will remain in my verse.

(Compare Nos. 5 and 6.)

54

Oh, how much more doth beauty beauteous seem
By that sweet ornament which truth doth give:
The rose looks fair, but fairer we it deem   3
For that sweet odor which doth in it live.
The canker blooms have full as deep a dye
As the perfumed tincture of the roses,   6
Hang on such thorns, and play as wantonly
When summer's breath their masked buds discloses;
But, for their virtue only is their show,   9
They live unwooed and unrespected fade,
Die to themselves. Sweet roses do not so:
Of their sweet deaths are sweetest odors made.   12
  And so of you, beauteous and lovely youth,
   When that shall fade, my verse distills your truth.

7. **Nor:** neither; **Mars his:** Mars's. This common Elizabethan form of the genitive is an erroneous expansion of *'s*, standing for the old *-es* inflection; **quick:** lively.

9. **all oblivious enmity:** destructive hatred of any sort.

10. **pace forth:** go forward; continue; **your praise shall still find room:** praise of you will always find a place.

12. **wear this world out to the ending Doom:** last till the world's end at Judgment Day.

13. **that:** when.

॥॥॥॥॥॥॥॥॥॥॥॥॥॥॥॥॥॥॥॥॥॥॥॥॥॥॥॥॥॥

An idea familiar from classical writers is expressed here: that commemoration in verse can impart an immortality that no monument of stone can match.

55

Not marble nor the gilded monuments
Of princes shall outlive this pow'rful rhyme,
But you shall shine more bright in these contents   3
Than unswept stone, besmeared with sluttish time.
When wasteful war shall statues overturn,
And broils root out the work of masonry,   6
Nor Mars his sword nor war's quick fire shall burn
The living record of your memory.
'Gainst death and all oblivious enmity   9
Shall you pace forth; your praise shall still find room
Even in the eyes of all posterity
That wear this world out to the ending Doom.   12
  So, till the Judgment that yourself arise,
    You live in this and dwell in lovers' eyes.

"Scripta manent." From Geoffrey Whitney, *A Choice of Emblems* (1586). The accompanying verse reads, in part:
    "Nothing at all but Time doth overreach;
     It eats the steel and wears the marble stone;
     But writings last, though it do what it can,
     And are preserved, even since the world began."

1. **love:** the poet addresses the emotion of love, probably that of the friend; **be it not:** let it not be.

2. **appetite:** lust.

3. **but today:** only for today.

4. **in:** to.

6. **wink:** close in sleep.

8. **dullness:** (1) sleepiness; (2) apathy.

9. **int'rim:** probably, separation.

10. **two contracted new:** a couple newly betrothed. Some commentators have been reminded of the tale of Hero and Leander, who were separated by the Hellespont.

<hr />

The poet presumably addresses his friend and pleads that he keep his love from being weakened by absence.

56

Sweet love, renew thy force; be it not said
Thy edge should blunter be than appetite,
Which but today by feeding is allayed,   3
Tomorrow sharp'ned in his former might.
So, love, be thou: although today thou fill
Thy hungry eyes even till they wink with fullness,   6
Tomorrow see again, and do not kill
The spirit of love with a perpetual dullness.
Let this sad int'rim like the ocean be   9
Which parts the shore where two contracted new
Come daily to the banks, that, when they see
Return of love, more blest may be the view;   12
  Or call it winter, which, being full of care,
    Makes summer's welcome thrice more wished,
    more rare.

1. **tend:** wait.

3. **no precious time:** i.e., none of his time is precious except that spent with the friend or in his service.

5. **world-without-end:** unending.

7. **think the bitterness of absence sour:** i.e., become sullen and resent the friend for causing the anguish of separation.

13. **true:** (1) real; (2) loyal; **fool:** (1) professional jester, hence, idiot; (2) plaything; **Will:** (1) whim; (2) more doubtfully, lust; (2) the poet himself.

⸻

As your slave, my time is entirely at your disposal and I cannot complain at waiting until you choose to see me, nor wonder what you are doing when we are apart, beyond thinking how fortunate are those in your presence. My loving folly is such that I can see no wrong in anything you do.

57

Being your slave, what should I do but tend
Upon the hours and times of your desire?
I have no precious time at all to spend,   3
Nor services to do till you require.
Nor dare I chide the world-without-end hour
Whilst I, my sovereign, watch the clock for you,   6
Nor think the bitterness of absence sour
When you have bid your servant once adieu.
Nor dare I question with my jealous thought   9
Where you may be, or your affairs suppose
But, like a sad slave, stay and think of nought
Save where you are how happy you make those.   12
    So true a fool is love that in your Will,
      Though you do anything, he thinks no ill.

"As love will." From Octavio van Veen, *Amorum emblemata*
(1608). The verse reads:
    "As the chameleon is, so must the lover be,
      And oft his color change like that whereon he stands;
      His lover's will his will, her bidding his command,
      And altered from himself right altered as is she."

3. **to crave:** should request.

4. **stay:** await; **leisure:** convenience.

6. **imprisoned absence of your liberty:** i.e., sense of being imprisoned I feel in your absence, which is made possible by your complete freedom to do as you like. It is possible that **liberty** also carries the sense of licentious behavior; compare No. 41.1.

7. **tame to sufferance:** trained to endure suffering; **bide:** endure; **check:** rebuff.

8. **injury:** injustice.

9. **list:** please; **charter:** privilege.

10. **privilege:** grant privilege to.

12. **self-doing crime:** (1) your own misdeeds; (2) the sins you commit against yourself.

13. **am to:** must.

<hr>

A repetition of the idea expressed in the preceding sonnet; a variation on the same theme.

58

That god forbid that made me first your slave
I should in thought control your times of pleasure,
Or at your hand the account of hours to crave,   3
Being your vassal bound to stay your leisure.
Oh, let me suffer, being at your beck,
The imprisoned absence of your liberty;   6
And, patience tame to sufferance, bide each check
Without accusing you of injury.
Be where you list; your charter is so strong   9
That you yourself may privilege your time
To what you will; to you it doth belong
Yourself to pardon of self-doing crime.   12
   I am to wait, though waiting so be hell,
    Not blame your pleasure, be it ill or well.

1. **nothing new:** compare Eccles. 1:9–10.

2. **beguiled:** cheated.

3. **invention:** new creation; **bear amiss:** miss their purpose in bearing.

4. **The second burden of a former child:** the same child a second time; the same old idea.

7–8. **some antique book/ Since mind at first in character was done:** i.e., old book dating back to that time when thought was first put into writing.

10. **composed wonder:** wonderful composition.

11. **mended:** improved; **whe'er:** whether.

12. **revolution be the same:** cf. the French saying "Plus ça change, plus c'est la même chose"; i.e., here, whether the cycle of time brings no change.

13. **wits:** thinkers; wise men.

꜏꜏꜏꜏꜏꜏꜏꜏꜏꜏꜏꜏꜏꜏꜏꜏꜏꜏꜏꜏꜏꜏꜏꜏꜏

If nothing new is possible, it is futile to labor to create novelty. Would that your image could be shown me in an old book, so that I could see whether we or the ancients excelled in describing you, or whether there has been any change at all. Certainly the sages of former times have admired less deserving objects than yourself.

59

If there be nothing new, but that which is
Hath been before, how are our brains beguiled,
Which, laboring for invention, bear amiss
The second burden of a former child!   3
Oh that record could with a backward look,
Even of five hundred courses of the sun,
Show me your image in some antique book,   6
Since mind at first in character was done:
That I might see what the old world could say   9
To this composed wonder of your frame;
Whether we are mended, or whe'er better they,
Or whether revolution be the same.   12
  Oh, sure I am the wits of former days
   To subjects worse have given admiring praise.

4. **In sequent toil all forward do contend:** toiling in orderly progression, all strive to move forward.

5. **Nativity:** the newborn child; **main of light:** main light of the world (from the dark womb).

7. **Crooked eclipses:** adversities.

8. **confound:** destroy.

11. **Feeds on the rarities of Nature's truth:** consumes those creations of Nature most admired for permanence.

12. **but for his scythe to mow:** except to be felled by his scythe.

13. **times in hope:** hoped-for times; the future.

|||||||||||||||||||||||||||||||||||||||

Human life moves on from birth to death as inevitably as the ocean's waves make for the shore. Time obliterates beauty and destroys everything that man regards as permanent; but my poetry in praise of you shall endure.

60

Like as the waves make toward the pebbled shore,
So do our minutes hasten to their end;
Each changing place with that which goes before,   3
In sequent toil all forward do contend.
Nativity, once in the main of light,
Crawls to maturity, wherewith being crowned,   6
Crooked eclipses 'gainst his glory fight,
And Time that gave doth now his gift confound.
Time doth transfix the flourish set on youth   9
And delves the parallels in beauty's brow,
Feeds on the rarities of Nature's truth,
And nothing stands but for his scythe to mow: 12
   And yet to times in hope my verse shall stand,
   Praising thy worth, despite his cruel hand.

8. **scope and tenor of thy jealousy:** sole subject of your suspicion.

11. **defeat:** overcome.

13. **watch I:** I remain wakeful; **wake:** stay up and revel.

14. **near:** intimate.

||||||||||||||||||||||||||||||||||||

Do you deliberately send your image to keep me wakeful through the weary night? Does your love spy on me thus suspiciously? No, it is my own love for you that ruins my sleep while you are enjoying pleasure elscwhere.

(Compare No. 27.)

61

Is it thy will thy image should keep open
My heavy eyelids to the weary night?
Dost thou desire my slumbers should be broken 3
While shadows like to thee do mock my sight?
Is it thy spirit that thou sendst from thee
So far from home into my deeds to pry, 6
To find out shames and idle hours in me,
The scope and tenor of thy jealousy?
Oh, no, thy love, though much, is not so great; 9
It is my love that keeps mine eye awake,
Mine own true love that doth my rest defeat,
To play the watchman ever for thy sake. 12
 For thee watch I whilst thou dost wake elsewhere,
 From me far off, with others all too near.

"Love never untroubled." From Octavio van Veen, *Amorum emblemata* (1608). The verse reads:
 "As billows on the sea against the rocks do beat,
  So thoughts both day and night perturb the lover's mind;
 For love right seldom can reposed quiet find,
  Because his restless thoughts his rest so ill entreat."

5. **gracious:** lovely and charming.

6. **true:** straight and well-proportioned; **no truth of such account:** no constancy so great.

8. **As:** as though.

10. **Beated:** battered; **chopped:** chapped; **tanned antiquity:** weathered old age.

11. **quite contrary I read:** I interpret quite differently.

12. **so self-loving:** loving itself under these circumstances: **were:** would be.

13. **my self:** my better self.

14. **days:** youth.

IIIIIIIIIIIIIIIIIIIIIIIIIIIIIIIIIIIIII

Love of self completely rules me and cannot be controlled, since it is deeply rooted in my heart. My face, my form, and my virtues surpass all others in my own esteem. But when I see my aged image in a mirror, I realize that it is you, my better self, that I love and praise.

62

Sin of self-love possesseth all mine eye,
And all my soul, and all my every part;
And for this sin there is no remedy,   3
It is so grounded inward in my heart.
Methinks no face so gracious is as mine,
No shape so true, no truth of such account,   6
And for myself mine own worth do define
As I all other in all worths surmount.
But when my glass shows me myself indeed,   9
Beated and chopped with tanned antiquity,
Mine own self-love quite contrary I read;
Self so self-loving were iniquity: 12
    'Tis thee (my self) that for myself I praise,
    Painting my age with beauty of thy days.

1. **Against:** forestalling the time when.
2. **o'erworn:** worn out.
5. **steepy:** steeply declining (like the setting sun).
10. **confounding:** destructive.
12. **my lover's life:** the life of my lover.
13. **black:** i.e., ugly.
14. **green:** be green (fresh and young).

‖‖‖‖‖‖‖‖‖‖‖‖‖‖‖‖‖‖‖‖‖

In anticipation of Time's destruction of my love's youthful beauty, I take steps to prevent its being forgotten. He shall live as young as ever in this verse.

63

Against my love shall be as I am now,
With Time's injurious hand crushed and o'erworn;
When hours have drained his blood and filled his   3
    brow
With lines and wrinkles, when his youthful morn
Hath traveled on to age's steepy night,
And all those beauties whereof now he's king   6
Are vanishing or vanished out of sight,
Stealing away the treasure of his spring—
For such a time do I now fortify   9
Against confounding Age's cruel knife,
That he shall never cut from memory
My sweet love's beauty, though my lover's life.   12
  His beauty shall in these black lines be seen,
    And they shall live and he in them still green.

1. **fell:** deadly; merciless.
2. **rich, proud cost:** splendid luxuries.
3. **sometime:** formerly.
4. **brass eternal slave to mortal rage:** brass designed to be everlasting subject to mortal violence (referring to destruction of memorial brasses by human hands).
8. **Increasing store with loss and loss with store:** adding to its store by the land's loss and adding to the land's loss by its increase.
9. **state:** condition.
10. **state:** (1) normal condition; (2) majesty, in senses "royalty" and "splendor"; **confounded to decay:** utterly destroyed.
14. **to have:** at having.

◾◾◾◾◾◾◾◾◾◾◾◾◾◾◾◾◾

Observation of the decay of splendid buildings and monuments designed to be eternal, and the way sea and earth alternate in possession of the land, has forced me to realize that Time will destroy my loved one. At this thought I cannot help weeping, because I fear to lose this precious possession.

64

When I have seen by Time's fell hand defaced
The rich, proud cost of outworn buried age,
When sometime lofty towers I see down-rased   3
And brass eternal slave to mortal rage;
When I have seen the hungry ocean gain
Advantage on the kingdom of the shore,   6
And the firm soil win of the wat'ry main,
Increasing store with loss and loss with store;
When I have seen such interchange of state,   9
Or state itself confounded to decay,
Ruin hath taught me thus to ruminate,
That Time will come and take my love away.   12
  This thought is as a death, which cannot choose
  But weep to have that which it fears to lose.

"The raging sea that roars with fearful sound,
  And threat'neth all the world to overflow,
The shore sometimes his billows doth rebound,
Though oft it wins and gives the earth a blow;
Sometimes where ships did sail it makes a land;
Sometimes again they sail where towns did stand."
    From Geoffrey Whitney, *A Choice of Emblems* (1586).

2. **sad mortality:** grievous destruction; **o'er-sways:** masters.

3. **rage:** violent action, as in No. 13, line 12; **hold:** maintain.

6. **wrackful:** destructive.

10. **Time's best jewel:** the most precious object of all time; **chest:** (1) strongbox; (2) coffin.

12. **spoil:** (1) loot; (2) ravage.

▪▪▪▪▪▪▪▪▪▪▪▪▪▪▪▪▪▪▪▪▪▪▪▪▪

Since neither brass, stone, earth, nor the mighty sea are proof against the ravages of Time, how can mortal beauty hope to withstand them! Since there is no defense against Time and no place to hide from him, the only possibility of preserving your beauty is in verse.

65

Since brass, nor stone, nor earth, nor boundless sea,
But sad mortality o'ersways their power,
How with this rage shall beauty hold a plea,　　　　3
Whose action is no stronger than a flower?
Oh, how shall summer's honey breath hold out
Against the wrackful siege of batt'ring days,　　　　6
When rocks impregnable are not so stout,
Nor gates of steel so strong but Time decays?
Oh, fearful meditation: where, alack,　　　　9
Shall Time's best jewel from Time's chest lie hid?
Or what strong hand can hold his swift foot back,
Or who his spoil of beauty can forbid?　　　　12
　Oh, none, unless this miracle have might,
　That in black ink my love may still shine bright.

2. **desert:** a deserving one.

3. **needy nothing:** the penniless nobody; **trimmed in jollity:** adorned in finery.

4. **unhappily forsworn:** maliciously denied; i.e., libeled.

6. **strumpeted:** called, or treated like, a strumpet.

7. **right:** true; **disgraced:** disfigured.

8. **limping sway:** unskillful management.

9. **art made tongue-tied by authority:** construed by some to refer to government censorship of the drama, but it could refer to pedantic strictures or other restrictions of the arts.

11. **simple truth:** pure honesty; **simplicity:** idiocy.

12. **captive good attending captain ill:** virtue enslaved to wickedness.

14. **to die:** by dying.

||||||||||||||||||||||||||||||||||||||

Wearied by the evils and injustices of this world, I long for the peace of death; but one thought deters me: I would have to desert my love.

66

Tired with all these, for restful death I cry:
As, to behold desert a beggar born,
And needy nothing trimmed in jollity,   3
And purest faith unhappily forsworn,
And gilded honor shamefully misplaced,
And maiden virtue rudely strumpeted,   6
And right perfection wrongfully disgraced,
And strength by limping sway disabled,
And art made tongue-tied by authority,   9
And folly (doctor-like) controlling skill,
And simple truth miscalled simplicity,
And captive good attending captain ill.   12
    Tired with all these, from these would I be gone,
    Save that, to die, I leave my love alone.

1. **infection:** corruption.

4. **lace:** adorn.

6. **dead seeming:** lifeless appearance; **of:** from; **hue:** (1) color; (2) general appearance.

7. **indirectly:** dishonestly.

8. **Roses of shadow:** shadowy (imaged) roses; artificial loveliness; **since:** seeing that.

9. **bankrout:** bankrupt.

11. **For:** because; **exchequer:** treasury.

12. **proud:** i.e., desirous to be **proud.**

13. **stores:** preserves as stock to draw upon.

‖‖‖‖‖‖‖‖‖‖‖‖‖‖‖‖‖‖‖‖‖‖‖‖‖‖‖‖‖‖‖

Why should my love live amid the corruptions of modern life, to grace evil? Why should his beauty inspire artificial imitation? Why should his life continue, now that Nature has poured all her treasure of beauty into him and must live upon his wealth? Nature is keeping him in reserve to exhibit as evidence of her former wealth of beauty.

67

Ah, wherefore with infection should he live
And with his presence grace impiety,
That sin by him advantage should achieve   3
And lace itself with his society?
Why should false painting imitate his cheek
And steal dead seeming of his living hue?   6
Why should poor beauty indirectly seek
Roses of shadow, since his rose is true?
Why should he live, now Nature bankrout is,   9
Beggared of blood to blush through lively veins,
For she hath no exchequer now but his,
And, proud of many, lives upon his gains?   12
    Oh, him she stores, to show what wealth she had
    In days long since, before these last so bad.

1. **map:** very picture of; pattern; **outworn:** past.
2. **as flowers do now:** i.e., naturally, in due season, without artificial prolongation.
3. **bastard signs of fair:** false semblances of beauty.
8. **gay:** splendid.
10. **itself and true:** constant to itself; unchanging.

━━━━━━━━━━━━━━━━━━━━

My love's beauty is thus like a representation of the past, when beauty took its natural course and was not assisted by artificial aids. For this reason Nature preserves him, to show the counterfeit beauty of today what true beauty was in former times.

68

Thus is his cheek the map of days outworn,
When beauty lived and died as flowers do now,
Before these bastard signs of fair were born   3
Or durst inhabit on a living brow;
Before the golden tresses of the dead,
The right of sepulchers, were shorn away   6
To live a second life on second head;
Ere beauty's dead fleece made another gay:
In him those holy antique hours are seen,   9
Without all ornament, itself and true,
Making no summer of another's green,
Robbing no old to dress his beauty new;   12
    And him as for a map doth Nature store,
    To show false Art what beauty was of yore.

2. **Want:** lack; **thought of hearts:** heartfelt (devoted) thought; **mend:** improve.

3. **the voice of souls:** i.e., that speak conscientious truth.

4. **Utt'ring bare truth, even so as foes commend:** saying no more than the bare truth, as people reluctantly praise their enemies.

5. **outward:** appearance; **outward praise:** superficial praise.

6. **give thee so thine own:** thus give you no more than your due.

7. **confound:** destroy.

14. **soil:** solution; reason; **dost common grow:** surround yourself with base companions.

⸻

Everyone praises your beauty with as much justice as one could wish. But when the world looks beyond your appearance to your character, praise is outweighed by criticism. The reason why your reputation is not as fair as your looks is that you are keeping bad company.

69

Those parts of thee that the world's eye doth view
Want nothing that the thought of hearts can mend;
All tongues, the voice of souls, give thee that due,　　3
Utt'ring bare truth, even so as foes commend.
Thy outward thus with outward praise is crowned;
But those same tongues that give thee so thine own　　6
In other accents do this praise confound,
By seeing farther than the eye hath shown.
They look into the beauty of thy mind,　　9
And that in guess they measure by thy deeds;
Then, churls, their thoughts, although their eyes were
　　kind,
To thy fair flower add the rank smell of weeds:　　12
　But why thy odor matcheth not thy show,
　The soil is this, that thou dost common grow.

3. **The ornament of beauty is suspect:** suspicion is the complement of beauty. Compare the proverb "Beauty and honesty [chastity] seldom agree."

5. **So:** provided that; **approve:** prove.

6. **being wooed of time:** since you are much sought after in these days.

7. **canker vice:** blight by the cankerworm.

8. **prime:** youth.

11. **so:** to such a degree.

12. **To:** so as to; **evermore enlarged:** ever again set free; always at liberty.

13. **masked:** shadowed.

14. **owe:** possess.

⁞⁞⁞⁞⁞⁞⁞⁞⁞⁞⁞⁞⁞⁞⁞⁞⁞⁞⁞⁞⁞⁞⁞⁞⁞⁞⁞

I shall not believe you guilty merely because you are accused, for beauty is ever suspected of unchastity. So long as you are innocent, false accusations only prove you the more virtuous, since such beauty as yours is sought by everyone and your youth is as yet unblemished. But your past virtue cannot protect you forever against slander. If you were not somewhat shadowed by suspicion, you would win all hearts.

70

That thou art blamed shall not be thy defect,
For slander's mark was ever yet the fair;
The ornament of beauty is suspect, 3
A crow that flies in heaven's sweetest air.
So thou be good, slander doth but approve
Thy worth the greater, being wooed of time; 6
For canker vice the sweetest buds doth love,
And thou presentst a pure unstained prime.
Thou hast passed by the ambush of young days, 9
Either not assailed, or victor being charged;
Yet this thy praise cannot be so thy praise
To tie up envy, evermore enlarged: 12
  If some suspect of ill masked not thy show,
  Then thou alone kingdoms of hearts shouldst owe.

"Love often deaf." From Octavio van Veen, *Amorum emblemata* (1608). The verse reads:
  "Whatever Fame bruits forth which tendeth to disgrace,
    Of Love's dear-prized love, he not endures to hear
    But makes himself be deaf by stopping either ear,
    To show he will not give to ill opinion place."

2. **surly:** dismal; **sullen:** mournful.
8. **woe:** woeful.
11. **rehearse:** repeat.
12. **decay:** be destroyed.

Mourn me no longer than you hear the bell toll for my passing. Even if you read this verse, forget the author. So much I love you that I would rather be forgotten than cause you grief. Do not even repeat my name if you reread this verse, but let your love die with me, lest people connect your tears with me and taunt you for your love.

71

No longer mourn for me when I am dead
Than you shall hear the surly sullen bell
Give warning to the world that I am fled   3
From this vile world, with vilest worms to dwell.
Nay, if you read this line, remember not
The hand that writ it, for I love you so   6
That I in your sweet thoughts would be forgot,
If thinking on me then should make you woe.
Oh, if, I say, you look upon this verse   9
When I, perhaps, compounded am with clay,
Do not so much as my poor name rehearse,
But let your love even with my life decay,   12
   Lest the wise world should look into your moan
   And mock you with me after I am gone.

1. **task you to recite:** give you the difficult task of reciting.

5. **virtuous:** powerful, with a pun on the other sense.

9. **false:** dishonest.

10. **untrue:** untruly.

13. **that which I bring forth:** perhaps a reference to his playwriting.

||||||||||||||||||||||||||||||||||||

Lest you be asked to justify your love for me, forget me when I am dead; you cannot truthfully credit me with worth. Therefore, lest your devotion turn you to dishonesty, let my name be forgotten and no longer shame either of us. For my works disgrace me and will bring disgrace upon you for loving worthless things.

72

Oh, lest the world should task you to recite
What merit lived in me that you should love,
After my death, dear love, forget me quite,   3
For you in me can nothing worthy prove;
Unless you would devise some virtuous lie,
To do more for me than mine own desert   6
And hang more praise upon deceased I
Than niggard truth would willingly impart.
Oh, lest your true love may seem false in this,   9
That you for love speak well of me untrue,
My name be buried where my body is,
And live no more to shame nor me nor you: 12
    For I am shamed by that which I bring forth,
    And so should you, to love things nothing worth.

4. **late:** lately.
10. **That:** as; **his:** its.
12. **Consumed with that which it was nourished by:** i.e., breath, air, which makes the fire burn.
14. **leave:** let go.

||||||||||||||||||||||||||||||||

In me you see the autumn of life, the twilight of day, which will soon yield to night. Seeing this, your love is strengthened for one whom you must soon lose.

73

That time of year thou mayst in me behold
When yellow leaves, or none, or few, do hang
Upon those boughs which shake against the cold,   3
Bare, ruined choirs where late the sweet birds sang.
In me thou seest the twilight of such day
As after sunset fadeth in the west,   6
Which by and by black night doth take away,
Death's second self that seals up all in rest.
In me thou seest the glowing of such fire   9
That on the ashes of his youth doth lie,
As the deathbed whereon it must expire,
Consumed with that which it was nourished by.   12
   This thou perceivest, which makes thy love more
      strong,
   To love that well which thou must leave ere long.

1. **fell:** ruthless.

2. **Without all bail:** not subject to bail.

3. **My life hath in this line some interest:** this verse to some degree is my claim to life.

6. **part:** i.e., of the poet's life.

7. **his:** its.

11. **The coward conquest:** (the body) being but a cowardly thing, vulnerable to the meanest wretch's knife.

13. **of that:** i.e., of the body; **that which it contains:** the spirit.

14. **this:** this verse.

||||||||||||||||||||||||||||||||||

But do not grieve when I am made prisoner by inexorable Death. Some part of me survives in this verse, which will stay with you. When you read this, you see my spirit, the better part of me.

74

But be contented: when that fell arrest
Without all bail shall carry me away,
My life hath in this line some interest   3
Which for memorial still with thee shall stay.
When thou reviewest this, thou dost review
The very part was consecrate to thee: 6
The earth can have but earth, which is his due;
My spirit is thine, the better part of me.
So then thou hast but lost the dregs of life,   9
The prey of worms, my body being dead,
The coward conquest of a wretch's knife,
Too base of thee to be remembered.   12
   The worth of that is that which it contains,
   And that is this, and this with thee remains.

1. **So are you:** you are exactly.
2. **sweet seasoned:** moderate and seasonable.
3. **peace:** pun on "piece," meaning a coin; **hold such strife:** i.e., maintain such a mental war.
6. **Doubting:** fearing.
14. **Or:** either.

              iiiiiiiiiiiiiiiiiiiiiiiiiiiiiiiii

You are as necessary to me as food to life or adequate rain to the earth. The pleasure of your love causes in me such anxiety as the miser feels, torn between enjoyment of his treasure and fear that it will be stolen. Thus I sometimes delight in having you to myself and at other times love to show you off; sometimes see you to my full content and other times starve for your sight. Having no delight except what I find in you, I alternate between feast and famine.

(Compare No. 52.)

75

So are you to my thoughts as food to life,
Or as sweet seasoned showers are to the ground;
And for the peace of you I hold such strife   3
As 'twixt a miser and his wealth is found:
Now proud as an enjoyer, and anon
Doubting the filching age will steal his treasure;   6
Now counting best to be with you alone,
Then bettered that the world may see my pleasure;
Sometime all full with feasting on your sight,   9
And by and by clean starved for a look,
Possessing or pursuing no delight
Save what is had or must from you be took.   12
   Thus do I pine and surfeit day by day,
    Or gluttoning on all, or all away.

1. **new pride:** novel adornment.
2. **quick:** lively.
3. **with the time:** according to fashion; **glance:** dart; **aside:** off the beaten path.
4. **compounds strange** new coinages of words or novel expressions.
6. **keep invention in a noted weed:** ever clothe my new creations in familiar garb (the same old language).
8. **where:** whence.
10. **argument:** theme.
11. **all my best:** the best I can do.
12. **spent:** (1) expended; (2) worn out.
14. **So is my love, still telling what is told:** so my love is renewed by continual repetition of its former expression.

▬▬▬▬▬▬▬▬▬▬▬▬▬▬▬

Why does my verse lack novelty and variation; why do I not turn to new methods of expression instead of writing always in the same way? Because my love for you is always my theme and the best I can do is to devise new arrangements for the old words. As the sun is daily reborn, so my love is freshened by continually repeating what I have said before. (Compare No. 108.)

76

Why is my verse so barren of new pride?
So far from variation or quick change?
Why, with the time, do I not glance aside   3
To new-found methods and to compounds strange?
Why write I still all one, ever the same,
And keep invention in a noted weed,   6
That every word doth almost tell my name,
Showing their birth and where they did proceed?
O, know, sweet love, I always write of you,   9
And you and love are still my argument;
So all my best is dressing old words new,
Spending again what is already spent: 12
   For as the sun is daily new and old,
   So is my love, still telling what is told.

2. **dial:** probably a sundial.

3. **vacant leaves:** i.e., of a tablet perhaps accompanying the sonnet as a gift to the friend.

6. **mouthed:** gaping; **memory:** reminder.

7. **shady stealth:** stealthily moving shadow.

8. **thievish:** stealthy; sneaky.

9. **Look what:** whatever.

10. **waste blanks:** empty pages.

11. **nursed:** cherished and developed.

12. **To make a new acquaintance of thy mind:** i.e., to seem new when you read them after a lapse of time.

13. **offices:** functions (of the glass, dial, and tablet); **look:** seek.

14. **enrich thy book:** enrich the thoughts that you note down in the book.

︙︙︙︙︙︙︙︙︙︙︙︙︙︙︙︙︙︙︙︙︙︙︙︙︙

A mirror will reflect your beauty's decay, a dial how your time is passing; the blanks of this book will hold your thoughts, which may cause you to read in the glass the inevitability of death and in the dial how inexorably time passes. Whatever you fear to forget, write on the blank leaves, and you will find that your thoughts improve on a second reading. The more you regard the glass and dial and their lessons, the more profound will be the thoughts you record in your book.

77

Thy glass will show thee how thy beauties wear,
Thy dial how thy precious minutes waste;
The vacant leaves thy mind's imprint will bear,   3
And of this book this learning mayst thou taste.
The wrinkles which thy glass will truly show,
Of mouthed graves will give thee memory.   6
Thou by thy dial's shady stealth mayst know
Time's thievish progress to eternity.
Look what thy memory cannot contain,   9
Commit to these waste blanks and thou shalt find
Those children nursed, delivered from thy brain,
To take a new acquaintance of thy mind.   12
  These offices, so oft as thou wilt look,
    Shall profit thee and much enrich thy book.

3. **As:** that; **alien:** unfamiliar; i.e., not in the addressee's circle of friends; **got:** adopted; **use:** habit.

4. **under thee:** under your patronage.

5. **dumb:** mute; **on high:** (1) conspicuously; (2) proudly.

7. **added feathers:** from falconry, referring to the practice of mending a bird's damaged wing with feathers to improve flight.

8. **given grace a double majesty:** made that which was only noble truly majestic.

9. **compile:** compose.

11. **mend:** improve.

12. **arts:** learning and skill; **graces:** virtues; **graced be:** are made more pleasing; i.e., what would otherwise be mere scholarly exercises of virtuosity are made more sweet and elegant.

13. **art:** learning; **advance:** elevate.

—————————————

I have dedicated my verse to you so often that others now also address their verse to you. Having already inspired this ignorant poet to flights of eloquence, you now add to the skill of the learned. You should be proud of my creations particularly, because they derive wholly from you. Your influence makes every work more pleasing; but all my skill and learning are due to you.

78

So oft have I invoked thee for my Muse
And found such fair assistance in my verse,
As every alien pen hath got my use   3
And under thee their poesy disperse.
Thine eyes, that taught the dumb on high to sing
And heavy ignorance aloft to fly,   6
Have added feathers to the learned's wing
And given grace a double majesty.
Yet be most proud of that which I compile,   9
Whose influence is thine and born of thee.
In others' works thou dost but mend the style,
And arts with thy sweet graces graced be;   12
   But thou art all my art and dost advance
   As high as learning my rude ignorance.

2. **grace:** (1) charm, excellence; (2) favor.

3. **my gracious numbers are decayed:** i.e., my poetry has lost its power to charm.

4. **give another place:** make way for another poet.

5. **thy lovely argument:** the lovely theme of you.

9. **lends:** offers.

11. **afford:** offer.

14. **what he owes thee thou thyself dost pay:** i.e., he should thank you for giving him the theme of his poetry rather than expecting thanks for his praise.

▃▃▃▃▃▃▃▃▃▃▃▃▃▃▃▃▃

When I was the only poet who addressed you, I received all your favor and inspiration. But now my powers of invention fail and another poet takes my place. Granted that you deserve to be celebrated by a more skillful pen, yet your poet only re-creates in his verse the virtue and beauty he sees in you. Don't thank him for his praise; his thanks are due to you.

79

Whilst I alone did call upon thy aid,
My verse alone had all thy gentle grace;
But now my gracious numbers are decayed,   3
And my sick Muse doth give another place.
I grant, sweet love, thy lovely argument
Deserves the travail of a worthier pen;   6
Yet what of thee thy poet doth invent
He robs thee of and pays it thee again.
He lends thee virtue, and he stole that word   9
From thy behavior; beauty doth he give,
And found it in thy cheek; he can afford
No praise to thee but what in thee doth live.   12
    Then thank him not for that which he doth say,
    Since what he owes thee thou thyself dost pay.

1. **faint:** falter.
2. **better spirit:** more talented poet.
4. **To make:** making.
6. **as:** as well as; **proudest:** most splendid.
7. **saucy:** presumptuous.
8. **willfully:** freely; at will.
10. **soundless:** fathomless.
12. **tall:** splendid; **pride:** magnificence.
14. **decay:** ruin.

Oh, how I lose heart in writing of you, knowing a greater talent is devoting his best efforts to your praise! But since your generosity is boundless, it will accept even a humble talent like mine that asks for little, while his rewards are great. I may be discarded as worthless, while his superiority will be approved. But if I had not loved you so much, I would not have relied solely on you and would not be threatened with utter destruction.

80

Oh, how I faint when I of you do write,
Knowing a better spirit doth use your name,
And in the praise thereof spends all his might   3
To make me tongue-tied, speaking of your fame.
But since your worth (wide as the ocean is)
The humble as the proudest sail doth bear,   6
My saucy bark, inferior far to his,
On your broad main doth willfully appear.
Your shallowest help will hold me up afloat,   9
Whilst he upon your soundless deep doth ride;
Or, being wracked, I am a worthless boat,
He of tall building and of goodly pride.   12
    Then if he thrive, and I be cast away,
    The worst was this: my love was my decay.

1. **Or:** whether.
3. **hence:** this world.
4. **part:** quality or accomplishment.
10. **o'erread:** read through.
11. **your being shall rehearse:** shall tell of your existence.
13. **still:** ever; **virtue:** power.

||||||||||||||||||||||||||||||||||||

No matter which of us outlives the other, death will not kill your memory, although everything about me will be forgotten. I shall have but a common grave, but you shall be ever before men's eyes, your monument my verse. Through the power of poetry your name will live forever on men's lips.

81

Or I shall live your epitaph to make,
Or you survive when I in earth am rotten,
From hence your memory death cannot take,   3
Although in me each part will be forgotten.
Your name from hence immortal life shall have,
Though I, once gone, to all the world must die.   6
The earth can yield me but a common grave,
When you entombed in men's eyes shall lie.
Your monument shall be my gentle verse,   9
Which eyes not yet created shall o'erread;
And tongues to be your being shall rehearse
When all the breathers of this world are dead: 12
  You still shall live (such virtue hath my pen)
   Where breath most breathes, even in the mouths of
    men.

2. **attaint:** stain of infidelity; **o'erlook:** look over; read through.

3. **dedicated:** devoted; possibly also, used in dedications.

4. **blessing every book:** i.e., the name of the fair subject, conferring grace (and prosperity) on every book dedicated to him.

5. **hue:** (1) complexion; (2) form.

6. **Finding thy worth a limit past my praise:** knowing yourself to be worthy beyond my power to praise.

7. **enforced:** forced.

8. **fresher stamp of the time-bettering days:** i.e., a newer model in poets, who will depict him in the style of the modern age, which constantly seeks to improve on the past.

10. **strained:** exaggerated.

11. **truly fair:** naturally and ideally lovely; **truly sympathized:** expressed with exact correspondence to truth.

13. **gross:** (1) coarse; (2) obvious; **painting:** flattery.

14. **abused:** used wrongly, because unnecessarily.

━━━━━━━━━━━━━━━━

True, you are not bound to read only my verse and may read the work of others. You know my talent cannot do you justice, and you seek a new model in poets who can describe you in more pleasing terms. Do so; yet whatever extravagant rhetoric such poets may invent, it cannot match in truth the picture painted by your faithful lover. Their artificiality would be more suitably applied to subjects lacking natural beauty.

82

I grant thou wert not married to my Muse,
And therefore mayst without attaint o'erlook
The dedicated words which writers use   3
Of their fair subject, blessing every book.
Thou art as fair in knowledge as in hue,
Finding thy worth a limit past my praise,   6
And therefore art enforced to seek anew
Some fresher stamp of the time-bettering days.
And do so, love; yet when they have devised   9
What strained touches rhetoric can lend,
Thou, truly fair, wert truly sympathized
In true plain words by thy true-telling friend: 12
   And their gross painting might be better used
   Where cheeks need blood; in thee it is abused.

2. **to your fair no painting set:** used no (1) artificiality; (2) flattery, in describing your beauty.

4. **barren tender of a poet's debt:** worthless offering that a poet feels obligated to make to his patron.

5. **slept in your report:** come short of praising you fully.

7. **modern:** commonplace, ordinary.

9. **silence:** reserve; **for my sin you did impute:** you considered to be a fault in me.

10. **Which:** i.e., the silence.

12. **life:** immortality; **a tomb:** an elaborate structure in which your true self is buried.

▬▬▬▬▬▬▬▬▬▬▬▬▬▬▬▬

It seemed to me that you were too beautiful to need exaggerated praise; I thought you surpassed anything a poet could say to earn your reward. Therefore I did not sufficiently exert myself to do you justice, since your living self can demonstrate the inadequacy of an ordinary pen in describing your worth. You thought the low key of my praise a fault, but it is to my credit that I do not mar your beauty with flattery, while others are burying it in elaborate conceits.

83

I never saw that you did painting need,
And therefore to your fair no painting set;
I found, or thought I found, you did exceed   3
The barren tender of a poet's debt:
And therefore have I slept in your report,
That you yourself, being extant, well might show   6
How far a modern quill doth come too short,
Speaking of worth, what worth in you doth grow.
This silence for my sin you did impute,   9
Which shall be most my glory, being dumb,
For I impair not beauty, being mute,
When others would give life and bring a tomb.   12
   There lives more life in one of your fair eyes
   Than both your poets can in praise devise.

1. **which:** who.
3. **immured:** enclosed; **store:** total supply.
4. **example:** show.
5. **pen:** (1) quill; (2) sty; enclosure.
8. **so:** in that way.
10. **clear:** (1) pure; (2) glorious.
11. **fame his wit:** make his ingenuity famous.
14. **on:** of; **makes your praises worse:** (1) cheapens the praise given you; (2) makes it harder to praise you to your satisfaction.

Who can praise you more highly than one who declares you incomparable, containing in yourself the pattern of a beauty that cannot be matched? It is a poor talent that cannot glorify the subject treated, but describing you merely as you are ennobles any account. If a writer can but copy exactly the glory Nature gave you, he shall earn universal fame for his ingenious invention. But your gracious endowments are accompanied by a fault: you dote on flattery. This makes you less praiseworthy and harder to praise.

84

Who is it that says most which can say more
Than this rich praise, that you alone are you,
In whose confine immured is the store 3
Which should example where your equal grew?
Lean penury within that pen doth dwell
That to his subject lends not some small glory; 6
But he that writes of you, if he can tell
That you are you, so dignifies his story.
Let him but copy what in you is writ, 9
Not making worse what Nature made so clear,
And such a counterpart shall fame his wit,
Making his style admired everywhere. 12
  You to your beauteous blessings add a curse,
  Being fond on praise, which makes your praises
    worse.

1. **in manners:** politely.

2. **comments of your praise:** elaborations of praise of you; **compiled:** composed.

3. **Reserve:** preserve; **character:** writing; **with:** by means of.

4. **filed:** polished.

6. **unlettered clerk:** illiterate parish clerk.

7. **that able spirit affords:** that any talented person offers.

12. **Though words come hindmost, holds his rank before:** i.e., though my words are inferior to those of others, my love yields to no one.

13. **breath of words:** airy, therefore inconsequential, words; **respect:** pay attention to. Proverbially, "Words are but wind."

14. **in effect:** in deeds.

||||||||||||||||||||||||||||||||||||||

I politely hold my tongue when you are being praised in polished terms full of learning. I think of you lovingly, while others write of their love, and dutifully give my approval to every verse from the skilled pen of an able poet. When I hear your praise, my tongue attests its truth, but I add something more in my heart, whose love for you is second to no one's, however inferior may be my words. So give ear to others' verbal praise—for what it is worth—but credit me with love expressed not in words but in deeds.

85

My tongue-tied Muse in manners holds her still,
While comments of your praise, richly compiled,
Reserve their character with golden quill   3
And precious phrase by all the Muses filed.
I think good thoughts, whilst others write good words,
And, like unlettered clerk, still cry "Amen"   6
To every hymn that able spirit affords
In polished form of well-refined pen.
Hearing you praised, I say, "'Tis so, 'tis true,"   9
And to the most of praise add something more;
But that is in my thought, whose love to you,
Though words come hindmost, holds his rank before.   12
    Then others for the breath of words respect,
    Me for my dumb thoughts, speaking in effect.

"Demonstration more effectual than speech." From Octavio van Veen, *Amorum emblemata* (1608). The verse reads:
  "Love rather is in deed by demonstration shown,
    Than told with sug'red words whose value is but wind;
    For speech may please the ear and not disclose the mind,
    But fraudless is the love whereas the heart is known."

1. **his:** a specific rival poet is presumed, Marlowe to those who believe Southampton the friend; George Chapman to those who prefer Pembroke. For a full discussion of the case for Chapman, see J. Dover Wilson, *An Introduction to Shakespeare's Sonnets* (New York, 1964), pp. 55–9.

3. **ripe:** ready for delivery.

5. **spirit:** genius; **spirits:** apparitions.

6. **pitch:** height.

7. **compeers:** associates.

8. **astonished:** struck dumb.

9. **affable familar ghost:** in Chapman's poem *The Tears of Peace*, the supposed spirit of Homer appears to him and claims to have inspired Chapman's translations of his works.

10. **gulls:** crams and dupes; **intelligence:** information.

13. **countenance:** (1) face; (2) favor; (3) patronage; **filled up his line:** made up for any deficiency in his verse.

━━━━━━━━━━━━━━━━━━━

Was it the proud confidence of his copious verse, designed to capture your favor, that silenced my thoughts before they were brought forth? Was it his genius, heightened by supernatural aid, that silenced me? No, neither he himself nor his assistants struck me dumb. When you became the subject of his verse and favored it, then I no longer had subject matter: that enfeebled my verse.

86

Was it the proud full sail of his great verse,
Bound for the prize of all-too-precious you,
That did my ripe thoughts in my brain enhearse,   3
Making their tomb the womb wherein they grew?
Was it his spirit, by spirits taught to write
Above a mortal pitch, that struck me dead?   6
No, neither he, nor his compeers by night
Giving him aid, my verse astonished.
He, nor that affable familiar ghost,   9
Which nightly gulls him with intelligence,
As victors of my silence cannot boast:
I was not sick of any fear from thence: 12
   But when your countenance filled up his line,
   Then lacked I matter; that enfeebled mine.

2. **like:** likely; **estimate:** value.

3. **charter:** privilege; **releasing:** freedom from obligation.

4. **bonds in thee:** (1) ties of affection in thee; (2) deeds entitling me to thee; **determinate:** ended.

7. **cause:** justification; **wanting:** lacking.

8. **patent:** title of possession; **back again is swerving:** is now reverting to you.

11. **upon misprision growing:** springing from error.

12. **on better judgment making:** upon your making a more accurate assessment.

13. **flatter:** encourage falsely.

‖‖‖‖‖‖‖‖‖‖‖‖‖‖‖‖‖‖‖‖‖‖‖‖‖‖‖‖

Farewell, you are too precious for me to possess, and no doubt you know your worth, which gives you the privilege of recalling your love. For I can only have you by your free gift, and, since I deserve nothing so rich, my right to possess you is at your disposal. You gave yourself to me, either not knowing your own worth or else mistaking mine; but your better judgment now recalls the gift. Thus I have had you as one dreams of being a king, only to awaken to reality.

87

Farewell: thou art too dear for my possessing,
And like enough thou knowst thy estimate.
The charter of thy worth gives thee releasing;   3
My bonds in thee are all determinate.
For how do I hold thee but by thy granting,
And for that riches where is my deserving?   6
The cause of this fair gift in me is wanting,
And so my patent back again is swerving.
Thyself thou gavest, thy own worth then not knowing,   9
Or me, to whom thou gavest it, else mistaking;
So thy great gift, upon misprision growing,
Comes home again, on better judgment making.   12
 Thus have I had thee as a dream doth flatter:
 In sleep a king, but waking no such matter.

1. **set me light:** esteem me little.
2. **place my merit in the eye of scorn:** regard my worth with a scornful eye, or cause others to do so.
4. **forsworn:** perjured, having broken their vow of friendship.
6. **Upon thy part:** on your behalf.
7. **attainted:** stained; tainted.
8. **That:** so that.
12. **vantage:** profit; **double vantage me:** provide a double profit in doing me good also.
14. **for thy right:** to justify you.

‖‖‖‖‖‖‖‖‖‖‖‖‖‖‖‖‖‖‖‖‖‖‖‖‖‖‖‖‖‖

Even though you choose to discredit me and scorn my worth, I will take your part, even if you have been faithless to our friendship. Best knowing my own faults, I can testify for you to the hidden flaws that blemish my own character, so that you may be applauded for disgracing me. At the same time, I shall also gain; since I love you beyond myself, the harm I do myself for your good will at the same time benefit me. I love you so much that I will assume any blame to protect you.

88

When thou shalt be disposed to set me light
And place my merit in the eye of scorn,
Upon thy side against myself I'll fight   3
And prove thee virtuous, though thou art forsworn.
With mine own weakness being best acquainted,
Upon thy part I can set down a story   6
Of faults concealed, wherein I am attainted,
That thou, in losing me, shall win much glory:
And I by this will be a gainer too;   9
For, bending all my loving thoughts on thee,
The injuries that to myself I do,
Doing thee vantage, double vantage me.   12
   Such is my love, to thee I so belong,
    That for thy right myself will bear all wrong.

1. **fault:** misdeed.
2. **comment upon:** add collaborative detail for.
3. **straight:** at once, with a pun on the other meaning.
4. **reasons:** arguments.
5. **ill:** secondary sense: unjustly.
6. **set a form upon desired change:** provide formal grounds for changing our relationship.
8. **acquaintance strangle and look strange:** choke off our friendship and pretend not to know you.
9. **walks:** haunts.
12. **haply:** perhaps.
13. **vow debate:** declare war.

If you claim to have deserted me for some wrong-doing, I will substantiate the charge; call me lame and I will limp at once; I will not contest your accusations. You cannot shame me half as much in justifying your desertion as I will shame myself, since you wish it. I will no longer claim your acquaintance; I will avoid your haunts and cease even to speak your name, lest I reveal our former friendship. I will declare war on myself, for I cannot be a friend to your enemy.

89

Say that thou didst forsake me for some fault,
And I will comment upon that offense;
Speak of my lameness and I straight will halt,   3
Against thy reasons making no defense.
Thou canst not, love, disgrace me half so ill,
To set a form upon desired change,   6
As I'll myself disgrace, knowing thy will;
I will acquaintance strangle and look strange,
Be absent from thy walks, and in my tongue   9
Thy sweet beloved name no more shall dwell,
Lest I, too much profane, should do it wrong
And haply of our old acquaintance tell.   12
  For thee, against myself I'll vow debate,
   For I must ne'er love him whom thou dost hate.

4. **drop in for an afterloss:** deal another blow when I am least expecting it.

8. **linger out:** lengthen; **purposed overthrow:** predestined destruction.

13. **strains:** sorts; **woe:** woeful.

||||||||||||||||||||||||||||||||||||||

Then hate me when you will, preferably now, when everything else is going badly for me. Do not wait until I have recovered from my present grief to inflict another one. If you are going to desert me, do so now; so I shall receive the worst blow of Fortune at once. Other griefs that seem painful will be nothing compared with the loss of you.

90

Then hate me when thou wilt—if ever, now—
Now, while the world is bent my deeds to cross,
Join with the spite of Fortune, make me bow,　　3
And do not drop in for an afterloss.
Ah, do not, when my heart hath scaped this sorrow,
Come in the rearward of a conquered woe;　　6
Give not a windy night a rainy morrow,
To linger out a purposed overthrow.
If thou wilt leave me, do not leave me last,　　9
When other petty griefs have done their spite,
But in the onset come: so shall I taste
At first the very worst of Fortune's might;　　12
　　And other strains of woe, which now seem woe,
　　Compared with loss of thee will not seem so.

1. **skill:** learning.
3. **newfangled ill:** fashionably ugly.
4. **horse:** a plural.
5. **humor:** temperament; **his:** its; **adjunct:** corresponding.
7. **particulars:** personal tastes; **measure:** satisfaction.
8. **one general best:** one possession that surpasses everything else.
10. **prouder than garments' cost:** more magnificent than showy garments.
12. **pride:** i.e., sources of pride.

⸻

Every man finds satisfaction in some personal possession—high birth, learning, wealth, physical strength, fine clothing, hawks, hounds, horses. I take no delight in such things but in something that surpasses them all: your love. In your love I have everything magnificent that men prize; I am poor only in this, that you may cease to love me and leave me completely wretched.

91

Some glory in their birth, some in their skill,
Some in their wealth, some in their body's force,
Some in their garments, though newfangled ill,   3
Some in their hawks and hounds, some in their horse.
And every humor hath his adjunct pleasure,
Wherein it finds a joy above the rest;   6
But these particulars are not my measure;
All these I better in one general best:
Thy love is better than high birth to me,   9
Richer than wealth, prouder than garments' cost,
Of more delight than hawks or horses be;
And, having thee, of all men's pride I boast—   12
  Wretched in this alone, that thou mayst take
   All this away and me most wretched make.

2. **life:** i.e., that of the poet; **assured:** certified (as by legal deed).

5. **the worst of wrongs:** i.e., utter loss by the friend's desertion.

6. **the least of them:** knowledge of coldness in the friend.

9. **inconstant mind:** deliberate inconstancy.

10. **Since that:** since; **revolt:** turning away; infidelity.

11. **title:** claim; **find:** ascertain as valid; i.e., how rightfully may I call myself happy!

＿＿＿＿＿＿＿＿＿＿＿

Do your worst to rob me of yourself: I am certain of you so long as I live; and my life will end with your love. So I am better off than one who must suffer your changing whims; you cannot be deliberately fickle to tease me, since you know it would kill me. How rightfully can I claim to be fortunate: in having your love and in the certainty that I will not live to suffer its loss! But the purest happiness is shadowed by fear: I will not necessarily know when you are faithless!

92

But do thy worst to steal thyself away,
For term of life thou art assured mine,
And life no longer than thy love will stay,   3
For it depends upon that love of thine.
Then need I not to fear the worst of wrongs,
When in the least of them my life hath end;   6
I see a better state to me belongs
Than that which on thy humor doth depend.
Thou canst not vex me with inconstant mind,   9
Since that my life on thy revolt doth lie:
Oh, what a happy title do I find,
Happy to have thy love, happy to die!   12
    But what's so blessed-fair that fears no blot?
    Thou mayst be false and yet I know it not.

2. **love's face:** the face of the loved one.

3. **seem love to me:** show love for me; **altered:** i.e., the object of love.

5. **For:** because.

8. **moods:** fits of anger: **wrinkles strange:** distant expressions.

14. **answer not thy show:** does not correspond to your appearance.

⸻

I shall live like a deceived husband, supposing you true. Your face will still seem to show love for me, although your heart has changed. Some people's faces show their change of heart by anger and distant looks; but your face always is sweet and loving, whatever your thoughts and feelings may be. Your loveliness is as deceiving as Eve's apple if you are not as sweet as you look.

93

So shall I live, supposing thou art true,
Like a deceived husband; so love's face
May still seem love to me though altered new,   3
Thy looks with me, thy heart in other place.
For there can live no hatred in thine eye,
Therefore in that I cannot know thy change;   6
In many's looks the false heart's history
Is writ in moods and frowns and wrinkles strange:
But heaven in thy creation did decree   9
That in thy face sweet love should ever dwell;
Whate'er thy thoughts or thy heart's workings be,
Thy looks should nothing thence but sweetness tell.   12
 How like Eve's apple doth thy beauty grow,
 If thy sweet virtue answer not thy show!

"Clear and pure." From Octavio van Veen, *Amorum emblemata*
(1608). The verse reads:
 "Even as the perfect glass doth rightly show the face,
  The lover must appear right as he is in deed;
  For in the law of love hath loyalty decreed
  That falsehood with true love must have no biding place."

1. **will do none:** do no deliberate hurt.

2. **most do show:** appear most capable of doing.

5. **rightly do inherit heaven's graces:** i.e., show themselves appropriate heirs of divine graces by their virtuous conduct.

6. **husband:** preserve; **Nature's riches:** beauty; **expense:** waste.

7. **their faces:** what they seem to be.

8. **stewards:** servants who handle the lord's affairs. The **excellence** entrusted to them is not theirs to be saved or spent at their own will.

10. **to itself it only:** only for and by itself; unprofitably.

12. **outbraves his dignity:** surpasses its fine appearance.

14. **Lilies that fester smell far worse than weeds:** this line also appears in the play entitled *The Reign of King Edward III* (1596), which has sometimes been attributed to Shakespeare. The idea is that of the proverb "Corruption of the best becomes the worst."

||||||||||||||||||||||||||||||||||||

Men who do not use their power to harm, who charm but are not charmed and are slow to be tempted—such men truly possess heavenly virtues and do not squander them. They exercise the self-control of true aristocrats and are served by other men, who dispense their favors. The summer flower is fragrant, even if it lives and dies unnoticed; but if it is attacked by cankerworm, the basest weed is more handsome. The best things become the worst by corruption.

94

They that have pow'r to hurt and will do none,
That do not do the thing they most do show,
Who, moving others, are themselves as stone, 3
Unmoved, cold, and to temptation slow:
They rightly do inherit heaven's graces,
And husband Nature's riches from expense; 6
They are the lords and owners of their faces,
Others but stewards of their excellence.
The summer's flow'r is to the summer sweet, 9
Though to itself it only live and die;
But if that flow'r with base infection meet,
The basest weed outbraves his dignity: 12
  For sweetest things turn sourest by their deeds;
  Lilies that fester smell far worse than weeds.

1. **lovely:** lovable.
6. **sport:** amorous adventures.
13. **large privilege:** great freedom (which his beauty makes possible).

━━━━━━━━━━━━━━━━━━━

How attractive you make the scandalous behavior that mars your youthful reputation! The gossip that reports your escapades praises you willy-nilly, because the very mention of your name clears his story of ill report. What a splendid house have those vices that infect you! Beauty cloaks every moral blemish and gives the whole a fair appearance. But beware of relying too much on this advantage; even the hardest knife will dull with overuse.

95

How sweet and lovely dost thou make the shame
Which, like a canker in the fragrant rose,
Doth spot the beauty of thy budding name! 3
Oh, in what sweets dost thou thy sins enclose!
That tongue that tells the story of thy days,
Making lascivious comments on thy sport, 6
Cannot dispraise but in a kind of praise;
Naming thy name blesses an ill report.
Oh, what a mansion have those vices got 9
Which for their habitation chose out thee,
Where beauty's veil doth cover every blot,
And all things turns to fair that eyes can see! 12
   Take heed, dear heart, of this large privilege;
   The hardest knife ill used doth lose his edge.

1. **wantonness:** libertinism.

2. **grace:** chief attraction; **youth and gentle sport:** amorous sport characteristic of a young gentleman.

3. **of more and less:** by those of high and low estates.

8. **translated:** transformed; **true:** honorable; **deemed;** judged.

9. **stern:** merciless.

11. **away:** astray.

12. **state:** regal splendor.

13-4. **But . . . report:** the same couplet as ends No. 36.

||||||||||||||||||||||||||||||||||||

Some accuse you of too much youthful amorousness; some say youthful dalliance becomes you; but everyone loves you. Your faults, like a cheap jewel on a queen's hand, are accounted honorable. If the cruel wolf could disguise himself as a lamb, how many lambs might he destroy! How many admirers might you lead astray, if you employed all your power to charm! But do not: I love you so much that I cherish your reputation as my own.

96

Some say thy fault is youth, some wantonness;
Some say thy grace is youth and gentle sport;
Both grace and faults are loved of more and less: 3
Thou makest faults graces that to thee resort.
As on the finger of a throned queen
The basest jewel will be well esteemed, 6
So are those errors that in thee are seen
To truths translated and for true things deemed.
How many lambs might the stern wolf betray, 9
If like a lamb he could his looks translate!
How many gazers mightst thou lead away,
If thou wouldst use the strength of all thy state! 12
   But do not so: I love thee in such sort
    As, thou being mine, mine is thy good report.

5. **removed:** i.e., of absence; **summer's time:** apposite to **teeming autumn,** i.e., the time when summer brought forth.

6. **teeming:** pregnant; **increase:** offspring; fruit.

7. **wanton burden of the prime:** luxuriant fruit conceived in spring.

11. **wait:** depend.

━━━━━━━━━━━━━

How winterlike has been the period of my absence from you! and yet it was the fruitful autumn, promising an abundant harvest that nevertheless seemed to me but poor consolation for the loss of you, the spring. For the joy of summer cannot come without you, and in your absence even the birds are still; or they sing with so little spirit that the leaves fade, fearing the approach of winter.

97

How like a winter hath my absence been
From thee, the pleasure of the fleeting year!
What freezings have I felt, what dark days seen!   3
What old December's bareness everywhere!
And yet this time removed was summer's time,
The teeming autumn, big with rich increase,   6
Bearing the wanton burden of the prime,
Like widowed wombs after their lords' decease:
Yet this abundant issue seemed to me   9
But hope of orphans and unfathered fruit;
For summer and his pleasures wait on thee,
And, thou away, the very birds are mute;   12
   Or, if they sing, 'tis with so dull a cheer
    That leaves look pale, dreading the winter's near.

2. **proud-pied:** splendidly multicolored; **trim:** fine array.

4. **That:** so that; **heavy Saturn:** Saturn, the planet associated with melancholy and sometimes with the personification of Time.

5. **nor . . . nor:** neither . . . nor; **lays:** songs.

6. **different flowers:** flowers different.

7. **any summer's story tell:** act (or speak) joyously.

8. **proud:** magnificent.

9. **wonder at:** admire.

11. **figures:** symbols.

14. **shadow:** image.

||||||||||||||||||||||||||||||||||||||

I have been absent from you in spring, when the loveliness of April can even make old Saturn caper gaily. But neither the birdsong nor the fragrance of many-colored flowers could delight me. I did not admire the white of the lily nor the deep red of the rose, those pleasant symbols of delight, except as they suggested you. It still seemed winter to me, because you were away. In your absence I amused myself by seeing your image in the flowers.

98

From you have I been absent in the spring,
When proud-pied April, dressed in all his trim,
Hath put a spirit of youth in everything,   3
That heavy Saturn laughed and leapt with him.
Yet nor the lays of birds, nor the sweet smell
Of different flowers in odor and in hue,   6
Could make me any summer's story tell,
Or from their proud lap pluck them where they grew:
Nor did I wonder at the lily's white,   9
Nor praise the deep vermilion in the rose;
They were but sweet, but figures of delight
Drawn after you, you pattern of all those.   12
   Yet seemed it winter still, and, you away,
   As with your shadow I with these did play.

"Absence killeth." From Octavio van Veen, *Amorum emblemata*
(1608). The verse reads:
   "Not to enjoy the sight of my fair lady's face,
   Makes nothing unto me to yield his true delight:
   The lily seemeth black, the sun to lack his light;
   Through absence of my love thus alt'red is the case."

1. **forward:** (1) presumptuous; (2) early.
2. **sweet that smells:** sweet scent.
3. **purple:** implying brilliance of color as well as the specific tone of one variety of violet; **pride;** splendor.
5. **grossly:** flagrantly.
6. **for:** i.e., for having stolen the hand's whiteness.
7. **buds of marjoram:** since marjoram flowers are purple, this may refer to the fragrance of the herb, which is compared to that of the friend's hair.
12. **pride:** prime.
15. **sweet:** fragrance.

IIIIIIIIIIIIIIIIIIIIIIIIIIIIIIIIII

I rated the spring violet for having stolen its scent from your breath and its brilliant color from your blood. I condemned the lily for stealing the whiteness of your hand and marjoram buds for their theft of the perfume of your hair. The guilty roses blushed or paled in fear; a red and white one had taken its scent from your breath and was punished in its prime when a cankerworm destroyed it. Other flowers I also saw, but all had stolen perfume and color from you.

99

The forward violet thus did I chide:
Sweet thief, whence didst thou steal thy sweet that
    smells,
If not from my love's breath? The purple pride   3
Which on thy soft cheek for complexion dwells
In my love's veins thou hast too grossly dyed.
The lily I condemned for thy hand;   6
And buds of marjoram had stol'n thy hair;
The roses fearfully on thorns did stand,
One blushing shame, another white despair;   9
A third, nor red nor white, had stol'n of both
And to his robb'ry had annexed thy breath;
But, for his theft, in pride of all his growth   12
A vengeful canker eat him up to death.
    More flowers I noted, yet I none could see
      But sweet or color it had stol'n from thee.   15

3. **fury:** inspirational frenzy; compare **rage**, No. 17, line 11.

4. **Darkening:** deadening; spending.

6. **gentle numbers:** genteel (aristocratic) verse; **idly:** vainly.

8. **argument:** theme.

9. **resty:** sluggish.

11. **satire:** satirist.

12. **spoils:** destructions.

14. **preventst:** forestallest; **crooked knife:** sickle; reaping hook; but **crooked** probably carries also the sense "malevolent," as in the **crooked eclipses** of No. 70, line 7.

ıııııııııııııııııııııııııııı

Where are you, my Muse of inspiration, that you so long have failed to celebrate the theme that makes you great? Is all your force devoted to trivial songs, debasing yourself to inspire low themes? Come back, Muse, and atone in noble poetry for the time so foolishly spent. Sing to him that honors your song and provides you with skill and theme. Regard my love's face; if Time has engraved any wrinkles there, become a satirist and make all the world hate his devastation. Glorify the fame of my love before Time destroys him; thus you forestall Time's weapons, which maim and kill.

100

Where art thou, Muse, that thou forgetst so long
To speak of that which gives thee all thy might?
Spendst thou thy fury on some worthless song,   3
Darkening thy pow'r to lend base subjects light?
Return, forgetful Muse, and straight redeem
In gentle numbers time so idly spent;   6
Sing to the ear that doth thy lays esteem
And gives thy pen both skill and argument.
Rise, resty Muse, my love's sweet face survey: 9
If Time have any wrinkle graven there,
If any, be a satire to decay
And make Time's spoils despised everywhere.   12
    Give my love fame faster than Time wastes life;
    So thou preventst his scythe and crooked knife.

Time, clipping Love's wings with his crooked knife. From Octavio van Veen, *Amorum emblemata* (1608).

2. **truth in beauty dyed:** i.e., one who is the personification of both truth and beauty.

3. **depends:** i.e., they would not exist at all if he did not exist.

4. **dignified:** thou (the Muse) art ennobled.

5. **haply:** perhaps.

6. **color:** adornment; **with his color fixed:** since its color is permanent.

7. **pencil:** brush (for the artist's skill); **lay:** apply.

13. **office:** duty.

▬▬▬▬▬▬▬▬▬▬▬▬

Wayward Muse, how shall you atone for neglecting the personification of truth and beauty? Perhaps you will answer that truth does not need glorification nor beauty an artist's skill, each being better left in its natural state. But will you be silent because he needs no praise? This will not do: through you he can live and be praised by posterity when his elaborate monument exists no longer. Then act your part, Muse, so that he will still appear in the distant future as he is now.

(Compare No. 14.)

101

O truant Muse, what shall be thy amends
For thy neglect of truth in beauty dyed?
Both truth and beauty on my love depends;   3
So dost thou too, and therein dignified.
Make answer, Muse: wilt thou not haply say,
"Truth needs no color, with his color fixed,   6
Beauty no pencil, beauty's truth to lay;
But best is best if never intermixed."
Because he needs no praise, wilt thou be dumb?   9
Excuse not silence so, for't lies in thee
To make him much outlive a gilded tomb
And to be praised of ages yet to be.   12
   Then do thy office, Muse, I teach thee how,
    To make him seem, long hence, as he shows now.

3. **That love is merchandised:** compare No. 21, line 14.

6. **wont:** accustomed.

7. **Philomel:** the nightingale, so named in mythology (Ovid, *Metamorphoses*, bk. vi); **front:** beginning.

8. **riper days:** the more mature summer.

11. **wild:** unrestrained.

12. **sweets:** delightful things; **dear:** hearty.

14. **dull:** bore.

‖‖‖‖‖‖‖‖‖‖‖‖‖‖‖‖‖‖‖‖‖‖‖‖‖‖‖‖‖‖‖

My love is stronger, though it may appear less: love is cheapened by being universally displayed. I first loved you in spring, and, like the nightingale, who sings in early summer and ceases at summer's height, I cease to sing your praises now that everyone else is doing so, because I do not wish to bore you.

102

My love is strengthened, though more weak in
    seeming;
I love not less, though less the show appear:
That love is merchandised whose rich esteeming   3
The owner's tongue doth publish everywhere.
Our love was new and then but in the spring,
When I was wont to greet it with my lays,   6
As Philomel in summer's front doth sing,
And stops her pipe in growth of riper days;
Not that the summer is less pleasant now   9
Than when her mournful hymns did hush the night,
But that wild music burdens every bough,
And sweets grown common lose their dear delight.   12
    Therefore, like her, I sometime hold my tongue,
    Because I would not dull you with my song.

1. **poverty:** poor stuff.

2. **such a scope:** so great a range; **pride:** grandeur.

3. **argument all bare:** unembellished theme.

7. **overgoes:** surpasses; **blunt:** (1) dull; (2) crude.

11. **pass:** result.

<hr/>

Alas, what poor stuff my Muse produces, when the theme is finer in itself than anything she can say of it! So do not blame me if I write no more; you can see in your mirror a face that quite surpasses my poor imagination, in comparison with which my lines, coarse and flat, shame me. It would be wicked to damage what is excellent in itself, and you are the only theme of my verses: your mirror can show you your image more truly than my verse can express it.

103

Alack, what poverty my Muse brings forth,
That, having such a scope to show her pride,
The argument all bare is of more worth   3
Than when it hath my added praise beside.
Oh, blame me not if I no more can write!
Look in your glass and there appears a face   6
That overgoes my blunt invention quite,
Dulling my lines and doing me disgrace.
Were it not sinful then, striving to mend,   9
To mar the subject that before was well?
For to no other pass my verses tend
Than of your graces and your gifts to tell;   12
   And more, much more, than in my verse can sit
   Your own glass shows you when you look in it.

4. **pride:** splendor.
6. **process:** progression.
7. **burned:** burned up; been consumed.
9. **dial:** timepiece.
10. **Steal from his figure:** (1) steal away from the friend's person; (2) move stealthily from its (the dial's) numerical position; **pace:** motion.
11. **hue:** appearance.
14. **beauty's summer:** the acme of beauty.

━━━━━━━━━━━━━━━━━━

You will never seem old to me, my lovely friend. Today, three years after I first saw you, your beauty seems unchanged. Nevertheless, you may be changing so imperceptibly that I am deceived; so I give notice to posterity: "You can never know what beauty is: the very flower of beauty died before you were born."

104

To me, fair friend, you never can be old,
For as you were when first your eye I eyed,
Such seems your beauty still. Three winters cold   3
Have from the forests shook three summers' pride,
Three beauteous springs to yellow autumn turned
In process of the seasons have I seen,   6
Three April perfumes in three hot Junes burned,
Since first I saw you fresh, which yet are green.
Ah, yet doth beauty, like a dial hand,   9
Steal from his figure and no pace perceived;
So your sweet hue, which methinks still doth stand,
Hath motion, and mine eye may be deceived.   12
    For fear of which, hear this, thou age unbred:
    Ere you were born was beauty's summer dead.

2. **show:** seem.

3. **Since:** because.

4. **still such, and ever so:** always the same theme and expressed in the same way.

6. **Still constant in a wondrous excellence:** ever true to his wondrous excellence; unalterably virtuous.

8. **leaves out difference:** omits variety.

9. **argument:** theme.

11. **change:** descant on one theme.

12. **affords:** makes possible.

14. **kept seat:** dwelled.

∎∎∎∎∎∎∎∎∎∎∎∎∎∎∎∎∎∎∎∎∎∎∎∎∎∎∎

Do not call mine an idolatrous love because I always sing hymns of praise to one person. This single-minded constancy is justified by the eternal excellence of my subject, who embodies the three verities of goodness, truth, and beauty, themes offering extraordinary scope for celebration. These virtues have often been found singly, but never until now, in my beloved, have all three appeared in one person.

105

Let not my love be called idolatry,
Nor my beloved as an idol show,
Since all alike my songs and praises be   3
To one, of one, still such, and ever so.
Kind is my love today, tomorrow kind,
Still constant in a wondrous excellence;   6
Therefore my verse, to constancy confined,
One thing expressing, leaves out difference.
"Fair, kind, and true" is all my argument,   9
"Fair, kind, and true," varying to other words;
And in this change is my invention spent,
Three themes in one, which wondrous scope affords.   12
   Fair, kind, and true have often lived alone,
   Which three till now never kept seat in one.

"Only one." From Octavio van Veen, *Amorum emblemata* (1608).
The verse reads:
   "No number else but one in Cupid's right is claimed;
   All numbers else besides he sets his foot upon;
   Because a lover ought to love but only one;
   A stream dispersed in parts the force thereof is maimed."

1. **wasted:** used up; past.
2. **wights:** humans, male and female.
5. **blazon:** description.
8. **master:** own.
10. **prefiguring:** picturing beforehand.
11. **for:** because; **divining:** speculative.
12. **skill:** knowledge.

⁙⁙⁙⁙⁙⁙⁙⁙⁙⁙⁙⁙⁙⁙⁙⁙⁙⁙⁙⁙⁙

When I read in ancient books of the beauties of former days, I realize that the authors meant to describe beauty like yours. Everything they say only prophesies you, whom they could not describe for lack of acquaintance. Even we today who behold you marvel but are tongue-tied when we attempt your praise.

106

When in the chronicle of wasted time
I see descriptions of the fairest wights,
And beauty making beautiful old rhyme,   3
In praise of ladies dead and lovely knights;
Then, in the blazon of sweet beauty's best,
Of hand, of foot, of lip, of eye, of brow,   6
I see their antique pen would have expressed
Even such a beauty as you master now.
So all their praises are but prophecies   9
Of this our time, all you prefiguring;
And, for they looked but with divining eyes,
They had not skill enough your worth to sing: 12
 For we, which now behold these present days,
  Have eyes to wonder but lack tongues to praise.

2. **on:** of.

3. **lease:** duration.

4. **Supposed as forfeit to a confined doom:** presumed subject to a definite termination.

5. **The mortal moon:** almost certainly Queen Elizabeth, often addressed as Cynthia (the moon-goddess) by poets. The **eclipse** may have been an illness that the Queen survived or her death, but better sense can be made from the latter.

6. **sad:** grave; mournful.

7. **Incertainties now crown themselves assured:** this may mean that the heir to the throne, before uncertain, has now been confirmed and crowned.

8. **peace proclaims olives of endless age:** peace promises a long continuance.

9. **balmy:** (1) peaceful; (2) having the property of soothing wounds, probably with reference to the oil used in the coronation ceremony.

10. **love:** i.e., affection for the friend; **subscribes:** yields.

12. **insults:** triumphs; **tribes:** multitudes.

░░░░░░░░░░░░░░░░░░░░░░░░░░░░

Neither my personal fears nor prophets of the future can control my love, presumed finite. Our queen has died, and those who prophesied disaster laugh at their own gloomy forecasts. A new monarch is crowned, and eternal peace is promised. The coronation oil has revived my love, and Death seems to submit to me, since I shall live in this verse, while he triumphs over the inarticulate many. And your memory shall endure in these lines when all memory of tyrants is gone.

107

Not mine own fears, nor the prophetic soul
Of the wide world, dreaming on things to come,
Can yet the lease of my true love control,   3
Supposed as forfeit to a confined doom.
The mortal moon hath her eclipse endured,
And the sad augurs mock their own presage;   6
Incertainties now crown themselves assured,
And peace proclaims olives of endless age.
Now, with the drops of this most balmy time,   9
My love looks fresh and Death to me subscribes,
Since, spite of him, I'll live in this poor rhyme,
While he insults o'er dull and speechless tribes: 12
   And thou in this shalt find thy monument
   When tyrants' crests and tombs of brass are spent.

1. **character:** write.
2. **figured:** portrayed; **true:** constant.
7. **Counting:** accounting.
8. **hallowed thy . . . name:** cf. "Hallowed be thy name" in the Lord's Prayer.
9. **in love's fresh case:** (1) in expressing love's case anew; (2) appearing like the ever-youthful personification of love.
10. **Weighs not:** has no care for.
11. **gives to necessary wrinkles place:** gives way before inevitable wrinkles.
13. **conceit:** conception; **bred:** newly born.

What idea that the pen can write has not already been expressed to portray to you my constancy? What new thing can be said to express my love or thy worth? Nothing: still, as though I were performing a holy office, I daily recite the same words—disregarding their age—describing our mutual love. Eternal love, ever fresh and youthful, pays no heed to the inevitable ravages of time and makes the same old phrases forever serve it, finding love's first rapture created anew in expressions whose age and archaic form suggest death.

(Compare No. 76.)

108

What's in the brain that ink may character
Which hath not figured to thee my true spirit?
What's new to speak, what now to register,   3
That may express my love or thy dear merit?
Nothing, sweet boy; but yet, like prayers divine,
I must each day say o'er the very same,   6
Counting no old thing old, thou mine, I thine,
Even as when first I hallowed thy fair name.
So that eternal love in love's fresh case   9
Weighs not the dust and injury of age,
Nor gives to necessary wrinkles place,
But makes antiquity for aye his page,   12
    Finding the first conceit of love there bred
    Where time and outward form would show it dead.

"Love is everlasting." From Octavio van Veen, *Amorum emblemata* (1608). The verse reads:

    "No time can ruin love; true love we must intend,
    Because not lasting still it hath not that esteem.
    The endless serpent ring unending time doth seem,
    Wherein love still remains from ever having end."

2. **flame:** ardor; **qualify:** temper; moderate.

5. **ranged:** strayed.

6. **travels:** i.e., makes a definite round-trip journey.

7. **Just:** punctual; **time:** hour; **not with the time exchanged:** not altered with the passage of time; or not changeable like time.

10. **blood:** temperaments.

11. **preposterously:** unnaturally; perversely (a stronger word than the modern sense).

━━━━━━━━━━━━━━━━━━

Never charge me with infidelity, though my absence may have suggested less ardent love; I might abandon myself as easily as my soul, which is in your breast. If I have strayed from you, it has only been like the traveler who makes a trip and returns punctually when expected, unchanged by his absence. Never think that, even if I were subject to every human frailty, I could err so perversely as to exchange for nothing all your worth. The whole universe holds nothing of value for me except you; you are everything to me.

109

Oh, never say that I was false of heart,
Though absence seemed my flame to qualify;
As easy might I from myself depart $\quad$ 3
As from my soul, which in thy breast doth lie.
That is my home of love: if I have ranged,
Like him that travels I return again, $\quad$ 6
Just to the time, not with the time exchanged,
So that myself bring water for my stain.
Never believe, though in my nature reigned $\quad$ 9
All frailties that besiege all kinds of blood,
That it could so preposterously be stained
To leave for nothing all thy sum of good: $\quad$ 12
   For nothing this wide universe I call
   Save thou, my rose; in it thou art my all.

2. **motley:** jester; **to the view:** in appearance. This may refer to acting, but the rest of the sonnet deals with infidelity. **Motley** could then symbolize the wearing of sundry colors as signs of allegiance to more than one love.

3. **Gored mine own thoughts:** in keeping with his motley appearance, perhaps, "divided my thoughts among several objects of affection."

4. **Made old offenses of affections new:** offended the former object of my love by forming new affections.

5. **truth:** constancy.

7. **blenches:** infidelities.

8. **worse essays:** trials of inferior loves.

9. **what shall have no end:** the poet's eternal love.

10. **grind:** whet.

11. **proof:** test.

12. **in love:** as an object of my love.

▬▬▬▬▬▬▬▬▬▬▬▬▬▬

It is true that I have behaved in a fickle fashion and treated love lightly, offending an older friend by making new ones. It is very true that I have disregarded the ideal of constancy; but, I swear by heaven, these infidelities only refreshed my heart and proved to me the worth of your love. This is all in the past: accept now my eternal devotion. Never again will I sharpen my love for you by experimenting with others; to you, the god of my love, I am bound. Then take me to your loving breast, the place I value next to heaven.

110

Alas! 'tis true I have gone here and there
And made myself a motley to the view,
Gored mine own thoughts, sold cheap what is most
    dear,   3
Made old offenses of affections new.
Most true it is that I have looked on truth
Askance and strangely; but, by all above,   6
These blenches gave my heart another youth,
And worse essays proved thee my best of love.
Now all is done, have what shall have no end: 9
Mine appetite I never more will grind
On newer proof, to try an older friend,
A god in love, to whom I am confined.   12
    Then give me welcome, next my heaven the best,
    Even to thy pure and most, most loving breast.

3. **life:** livelihood.

4. **public means:** i.e., a public career in the theatre; **public manners:** conformity to common taste.

8. **renewed:** restored.

10. **Potions of eisel:** draughts of vinegar (considered a plague remedy).

12. **Nor double penance to correct correction:** i.e., nor will I consider double penance excessive with the result that my spirit becomes resentful rather than being improved.

||||||||||||||||||||||||||||||||||||||||||

If you love me, take Fortune to task that I am forced to support myself by a public career that brings me to low estate. This disgraces my name and debases me to the common level. So pity me and hope for my redemption; I will humbly undergo any penance —pity me, and your mere pity will restore me to myself.

111

Oh, for my sake do you with Fortune chide,
The guilty goddess of my harmful deeds,
That did not better for my life provide   3
Than public means, which public manners breeds.
Thence comes it that my name receives a brand;
And almost thence my nature is subdued   6
To what it works in, like the dyer's hand:
Pity me then, and wish I were renewed,
Whilst, like a willing patient, I will drink   9
Potions of eisel 'gainst my strong infection;
No bitterness that I will bitter think,
Nor double penance to correct correction.   12
    Pity me then, dear friend, and, I assure ye,
     Even that your pity is enough to cure me.

1. **impression:** i.e., mark of a branding iron, with which some criminals were stamped.

2. **vulgar scandal:** the disgrace of being a common performer.

4. **o'ergreen:** cover over; refurbish; **allow:** acknowledge.

7. **None else to me, nor I to none alive:** no one else conscious of my true nature, and I conscious of no one else.

8. **That:** so that.

10. **adder's sense:** deafened ears; cf. Psalm 58:4.

12. **with my neglect I do dispense:** I justify my inattention.

13. **You are so strongly in my purpose bred:** you are so much the cherished aim of every endeavor.

||||||||||||||||||||||||||||||||||||||

Your loving pity heals my shame; why should I care for anyone else's censure, so long as you gloss over my misdeeds and call me good? You are all the world to me, and I cannot but regard your praise and blame as absolute; no one else can influence me. I am so indifferent to others' judgments that it is as though my ear were deaf. Behold my justification: you are the motive of everything I do, so that the world seems to hold no other living person.

112

Your love and pity doth the impression fill
Which vulgar scandal stamped upon my brow;
For what care I who calls me well or ill,   3
So you o'ergreen my bad, my good allow?
You are my all-the-world, and I must strive
To know my shames and praises from your tongue;   6
None else to me, nor I to none alive,
That my steeled sense or changes right or wrong.
In so profound abysm I throw all care   9
Of others' voices that my adder's sense
To critic and to flatterer stopped are.
Mark how with my neglect I do dispense: 12
   You are so strongly in my purpose bred
   That all the world besides methinks are dead.

1. **mine eye is in my mind:** i.e., I constantly behold the mental image of you.

3. **Doth part his function:** functions only partly.

4. **Seems seeing:** appears to see; **effectually:** in effect; **out:** blind.

5. **heart:** mind.

6. **latch:** catch sight of.

7. **his:** its (the eye's); **quick:** fleeting; **no part:** no awareness.

9. **rudest:** most unpolished; **gentlest:** most elegant.

10. **favor:** face; appearance.

12. **feature:** likeness.

13. **Incapable:** unable to hold.

14. **true:** faithful; **untrue:** false.

〰〰〰〰〰〰〰〰〰〰〰〰〰〰〰

Away from you, my vision is turned inward and only partly functions, since nothing I see makes any impression on my mind. Everything my eye beholds is transformed to your image, and, since it can hold nothing else, my faithful mind thus makes my vision faithless to its function.

113

Since I left you, mine eye is in my mind,
And that which governs me to go about
Doth part his function and is partly blind,   3
Seems seeing, but effectually is out.
For it no form delivers to the heart
Of bird, of flow'r, or shape which it doth latch;   6
Of his quick objects hath the mind no part,
Nor his own vision holds what it doth catch;
For if it see the rudest or gentlest sight,   9
The most sweet favor or deformed'st creature,
The mountain or the sea, the day or night,
The crow or dove, it shapes them to your feature.   12
   Incapable of more, replete with you,
    My most true mind thus maketh mine eye untrue.

1. **Or whether doth:** i.e., is it that; **crowned:**
(1) made regal; (2) filled to overflowing.

2. **flattery:** pleasant falsehood.

5. **monsters:** monstrosities; **indigest:** undigested;
formless.

8. **to his beams assemble:** come together before
the eye.

11. **his gust:** the mind's taste; **'greeing:** agreeing.

14. **doth first begin:** like a royal taster, takes the
first sip.

Is it because my mind, full of your majesty, has the
monarch's taste for pleasing deceptions, or does my
eye really see these things, taught by your love to
transform every object, however ugly, into your
image? It is the first of these—the enhancement of
what I see to please my mind, which accepts it like
a true king. Although my eye, to please my mind, may
offer it a poisonous draught, the eye should not be
blamed too much, since it willingly sips it first.

114

Or whether doth my mind, being crowned with you,
Drink up the monarch's plague, this flattery?
Or whether shall I say mine eye saith true,   3
And that your love taught it this alchemy,
To make of monsters and things indigest
Such cherubins as your sweet self resemble,   6
Creating every bad a perfect best
As fast as objects to his beams assemble?
Oh, 'tis the first; 'tis flatt'ry in my seeing,   9
And my great mind most kingly drinks it up:
Mine eye well knows what with his gust is 'greeing,
And to his palate doth prepare the cup.   12
  If it be poisoned, 'tis the lesser sin
    That mine eye loves it and doth first begin.

2. **Even those:** those very ones.

4. **most full:** very full.

5. **But reckoning:** only taking account of; **millioned accidents:** innumerable events.

7. **Tan:** weather; **intents:** intentions.

8. **Divert strong minds to the course of alt'ring things:** cause the firmest convictions to change with the time.

11. **certain o'er incertainty:** positive beyond all doubt.

12. **Crowning:** hailing as supreme.

13. **might I not:** I could not; **so:** i.e., the statement in line 10.

14. **To:** in order to; **still:** ever.

⁜⁜⁜⁜⁜⁜⁜⁜⁜⁜⁜⁜⁜⁜⁜⁜⁜⁜⁜⁜⁜⁜⁜⁜⁜

Those lines in which I said I could not love you dearer have proved untrue; but then I could not believe that my ardor could grow—thinking only of Time and its way of altering everything. This being the case, why shouldn't I have said, "Now I love you best," being positive that the present moment was supreme and the future doubtful? I should not have said so because Love is a babe, and the statement denied it inevitable growth.

115

Those lines that I before have writ do lie,
Even those that said I could not love you dearer;
Yet then my judgment knew no reason why   3
My most full flame should afterward burn clearer.
But reckoning Time, whose millioned accidents
Creep in 'twixt vows and change decrees of kings,   6
Tan sacred beauty, blunt the sharp'st intents,
Divert strong minds to the course of alt'ring things!
Alas, why, fearing of Time's tyranny,   9
Might I not then say, "Now I love you best,"
When I was certain o'er incertainty,
Crowning the present, doubting of the rest?   12
    Love is a babe; then might I not say so,
      To give full growth to that which still doth grow.

1. **true:** faithful.
4. **bends:** inclines.
5. **mark:** seamark; hence, guide.
8. **Whose worth's unknown:** whose influence is incalculable (referring to the star).
9. **fool:** plaything.
10. **bending:** curving; **compass:** reach.
12. **bears it out:** endures.
13. **upon me proved:** proved by my example.

May I at least never admit that anything can sever the ties of faithful lovers! The true lover does not change when his loved one does nor consent to separation. True love is as constant as the North Star. Love is not controlled by Time, although beauty is at its mercy; love does not change, like the quick passage of time, but lasts till Judgment Day. If this is untrue, and my own case proves it, then these words were never written, and true love has never existed.

116

Let me not to the marriage of true minds
Admit impediments; love is not love
Which alters when it alteration finds,   3
Or bends with the remover to remove.
Oh, no, it is an ever-fixed mark,
That looks on tempests and is never shaken;   6
It is the star to every wand'ring bark,
Whose worth's unknown, although his height be
    taken.
Love's not Time's fool, though rosy lips and cheeks   9
Within his bending sickle's compass come;
Love alters not with his brief hours and weeks,
But bears it out even to the edge of Doom.   12
    If this be error, and upon me proved,
    I never writ, nor no man ever loved.

"Nothing hindereth love." From Octavio van Veen, *Amorum
emblemata* (1608). The verse reads:
    "None else but Cupid can put back the term of love,
    To which all must give place, yea, Jove himself and all,
    Each being by his power brought in subjective thrall,
    Save only love itself, which force may not remove."

1. **scanted:** neglected.
3. **upon your dearest love to call:** to pay homage to your precious love.
5. **frequent:** intimate; **unknown minds:** bare acquaintances.
6. **given to time your own dear-purchased right:** occupied myself with whatever the passing moment offered, instead of devoting myself to you as I should in requital of your love.
9. **Book . . . down:** record.
10. **on:** on top of; **just:** precise.
11. **level:** range.
13. **prove:** test.
14. **virtue:** strength.

<hr/>

You may rightly accuse me of failing to requite you worthily and forgetting to say how precious your love is to me; that I have hobnobbed with near-strangers and frittered away my time instead of spending it with you, who have earned all my devotion by your love. Record both my accidental and my deliberate wrongs to you and add to my proven faults everything you can imagine against me; frown upon me; but do not make me the target of your hatred. I was merely testing the strength and constancy of your love.

117

Accuse me thus: that I have scanted all
Wherein I should your great deserts repay;
Forgot upon your dearest love to call, 3
Whereto all bonds do tie me day by day;
That I have frequent been with unknown minds
And given to time your own dear-purchased right; 6
That I have hoisted sail to all the winds
Which should transport me farthest from your sight.
Book both my willfulness and errors down, 9
And on just proof surmise accumulate;
Bring me within the level of your frown,
But shoot not at me in your wakened hate: 12
  Since my appeal says I did strive to prove
  The constancy and virtue of your love.

1. **Like:** just.
2. **eager:** sharp; piquant.
3. **prevent:** forestall; **unseen:** not yet showing symptoms.
6. **frame:** adapt.
7. **sick of welfare:** sated with health; **meetness:** suitability.
9. **policy:** cunning.
10. **faults assured:** real ailments.
11. **brought to medicine a healthful state:** reduced a healthful state to the need of medicine.
12. **rank of:** too highly fed with; **would by ill be cured:** sought a cure in illness.
14. **so:** thus.

||||||||||||||||||||||||||||||||||||

Just as we whet our appetites with sharp condiments and take purges to prevent sickness suspected rather than evident—just so, I sought evil companions to enhance the pleasure of your friendship and, overfull of happiness, thought it desirable to sample the misery of separation from you before it was really necessary. But the result of thus cleverly trying to prevent unhappiness made me really wretched; from which I learn that there is no cure for love of you that is not worse than the disease.

118

Like as, to make our appetites more keen,
With eager compounds we our palate urge;
As, to prevent our maladies unseen,   3
We sicken to shun sickness when we purge:
Even so, being full of your ne'er-cloying sweetness,
To bitter sauces did I frame my feeding;   6
And, sick of welfare, found a kind of meetness
To be diseased ere that there was true needing.
Thus policy in love, t'anticipate   9
The ills that were not, grew to faults assured,
And brought to medicine a healthful state,
Which, rank of goodness, would by ill be cured.   12
    But thence I learn, and find the lesson true,
    Drugs poison him that so fell sick of you.

2. **limbecks:** alembics; stills.

4. **losing when I saw myself to win:** i.e., gaining what turned out to be worthless: a base woman.

7. **spheres:** (1) sockets; (2) orbits; **fitted:** forced.

8. **madding:** maddening.

10. **better is by evil still made better:** better things are made to seem even more superior by contrast with evil.

13. **content:** true satisfaction.

||||||||||||||||||||||||||||||||||

How often have I been charmed by the wiles of an evil woman and wavered between hope and fear until I seemed to win her, only to find I had no prize! How often have I sinned when I thought myself blessed! And how often have my eyes been diverted by passion from their proper object of regard! But good has come from this evil: now I realize that what is excellent seems even better after experience of baseness and that love is stronger after reconciliation. Thus, corrected, I return to my true happiness and gain more than I have lost.

119

What potions have I drunk of Siren tears,
Distilled from limbecks foul as hell within,
Applying fears to hopes and hopes to fears,   3
Still losing when I saw myself to win!
What wretched errors hath my heart committed,
Whilst it hath thought itself so blessed never!   6
How have mine eyes out of their spheres been fitted
In the distraction of this madding fever!
O benefit of ill: now I find true   9
That better is by evil still made better;
And ruined love, when it is built anew,
Grows fairer than at first, more strong, far greater.   12
    So I return rebuked to my content,
    And gain by ills thrice more than I have spent.

"Love's tears are his testimonies." From Octavio van Veen, *Amorum emblemata* (1608). The verse reads:

"The tears of Love do serve for witnessing his woe;
His ardent love the fire, the furnace is his heart;
The wind that blows it, sighs, that rise from inward smart;
The limbeck his two eyes, from whence his tears do flow."

1. **unkind:** alienated (by another love).
7. **tyrant:** cruel oppressor; **leisure:** time.
8. **in your crime:** by your wrong to me.
9. **rememb'red:** reminded.
11. **tend'red:** offered.
12. **humble salve:** apology; **fits:** suits.
13. **that your trespass:** that trespass of yours; **fee:** payment.
14. **ransoms:** purchases freedom from punishment.

‖‖‖‖‖‖‖‖‖‖‖‖‖‖‖‖‖‖‖‖‖‖‖‖‖‖‖‖‖

That you once slighted me for another love helps me now. Because of the sorrow I felt then I cannot but submit myself humbly for my own wrong to you. For if you have suffered as I did, you have been through hell; and I cruelly failed to consider the misery I once knew in similar circumstances. That period of estrangement should have reminded my heart how keenly true sorrow is felt and caused me to offer you the prompt apology needed to ease a wounded heart. But that earlier fault of yours rewards me now: my fault excuses yours, and yours must excuse me.

120

That you were once unkind befriends me now,
And for that sorrow which I then did feel
Needs must I under my transgression bow, 3
Unless my nerves were brass or hammered steel.
For if you were by my unkindness shaken,
As I by yours, you've passed a hell of time, 6
And I, a tyrant, have no leisure taken
To weigh how once I suffered in your crime.
Oh, that our night of woe might have rememb'red 9
My deepest sense how hard true sorrow hits,
And soon to you, as you to me then, tend'red
The humble salve which wounded bosoms fits! 12
  But that your trespass now becomes a fee:
   Mine ransoms yours, and yours must ransom me.

2. **not to be:** not being vile.

3. **just:** lawful.

5. **adulterate:** (1) adulterous; (2) debased.

6. **Give salutation to:** assume familiarity with; **sportive:** erotic.

8. **in their wills:** in the light of their own lustful natures.

9. **that:** what; **level:** aim; guess.

10. **abuses:** faults.

11. **bevel:** crooked.

12. **rank:** corrupt; specifically, licentious; **shown:** portrayed.

13. **maintain:** assert.

ıılıllılılılılılılılılılılıllılılılılılı

One had better be depraved than be unjustly charged with vice, censured for vile acts one hasn't even performed, that one considers lawful pleasures anyway. Why should men of corrupt vision think they can identify the erotic bent of my nature; or why should those more prone to sin than I spy out my doings and judge them in the light of their own wanton tastes? I am what I am, not what they think me to be; in assessing me, they attribute to me their own vices, of which I may not be guilty. I should not be represented by their foul minds, unless they uphold this doctrine of universal wickedness: "All men are bad and are ruled by the evil in their natures."

121

'Tis better to be vile than vile esteemed,
When not to be receives reproach of being,
And the just pleasure lost, which is so deemed   3
Not by our feeling but by others' seeing.
For why should others' false adulterate eyes
Give salutation to my sportive blood?   6
Or on my frailties why are frailer spies,
Which in their wills count bad what I think good?
No, I am that I am; and they that level   9
At my abuses reckon up their own:
I may be straight though they themselves be bevel;
By their rank thoughts my deeds must not be shown,   12
  Unless this general evil they maintain:
  All men are bad and in their badness reign.

1. **tables:** (1) notebook; (2) pictures.

2. **Full charactered:** written in full.

3. **above:** beyond; **idle rank:** empty array of pages.

6. **Have faculty by Nature to subsist:** are empowered by Nature to live.

7. **rased oblivion:** oblivion, which erases everything.

8. **missed:** lacked; lost.

9. **retention:** container (the tables).

10. **tallies:** sticks on which accounts were scored.

12. **those tables:** i.e., of the mind; **more:** i.e., more fully.

13. **adjunct:** aid.

॥॥॥॥॥॥॥॥॥॥॥॥॥॥॥॥॥॥॥॥॥

The notebook, your remembrance, is impressed in my mind, where it shall be eternal—at least as lasting as my brain and heart; until they yield to death, the memory of you will remain. The notebook could never hold so much of you, nor do I need records of your love like a tavernkeeper. Thus I gave away the book, preferring to use the tables of memory, which retain you more perfectly. Using an aid to remember you would suggest that I was able to forget you.

122

Thy gift, thy tables, are within my brain
Full charactered with lasting memory,
Which shall above that idle rank remain   3
Beyond all date, even to eternity;
Or, at the least, so long as brain and heart
Have faculty by Nature to subsist,   6
Till each to rased oblivion yield his part
Of thee, thy record never can be missed.
That poor retention could not so much hold,   9
Nor need I tallies thy dear love to score;
Therefore to give them from me was I bold,
To trust those tables that receive thee more.   12
   To keep an adjunct to remember thee
   Were to import forgetfulness in me.

2. **pyramids:** despite conjectures that these were ancient obelisks newly set up in Rome, or those adorning triumphal arches for King James I in 1604, these are probably not man-made structures but natural forms such as mountains.

4. **dressings of a former sight:** new arrayals of what existed in the past.

5. **dates:** lifetimes; **admire:** wonder at.

7. **make them:** interpret them as; **born to our desire:** newly created for our pleasure.

8. **heard them told:** heard tell of them.

12. **haste:** speed in passing.

Time, I defy you to claim that I change! To me all your works are old creations newly dressed. Because men's lives are short, we do not realize the true age of the creations you palm off on us as new and accept them as made for us, instead of recognizing them. Neither you nor your chronicles inspire me with awe; both your records and your works are misrepresentations, which we are unable to identify because of the speed with which you hurry us through life. But this I vow: I will be constant, despite you and your threat of destruction.

(Compare No. 59.)

123

No, Time, thou shalt not boast that I do change:
Thy pyramids built up with newer might
To me are nothing novel, nothing strange;   3
They are but dressings of a former sight:
Our dates are brief, and therefore we admire
What thou dost foist upon us that is old,   6
And rather make them born to our desire
Than think that we before have heard them told.
Thy registers and thee I both defy,   9
Not wond'ring at the present nor the past;
For thy records and what we see doth lie,
Made more or less by thy continual haste.   12
    This I do vow, and this shall ever be:
    I will be true, despite thy scythe and thee.

1. **love:** i.e., for the friend; **but:** only; **child of state:** product of worldly condition.

2. **for Fortune's bastard be unfathered:** be considered the fatherless child of fickle Fortune.

5. **accident:** (1) Fortune; (2) mere chance.

6-7. **falls/ Under the blow of thralled discontent:** succumbs to resentment at its bondage.

8. **Whereto the inviting time our fashion calls:** to which fate the age invites men like us.

9. **Policy:** expedience; **heretic:** faithless one.

11. **all alone:** uniquely; **hugely politic:** enormously wise.

12. **That:** in that.

13. **fools of Time:** those who serve Time instead of eternal values; the worldly wise.

14. **Which die for goodness, who have lived for crime:** who, having been sinners, repent on their deathbeds.

<hr>

If my love sprang only from your position, it might be said to derive from your fortune and depend on the continuance of your prosperity. No, it is not based on such uncertainty; it is not affected by good fortune nor killed by resentment at being enslaved, as is often the case. It does not fear betrayal by false expedience, which is effective only during the brief span of life, but is the only thing truly wise, in that it remains the same in prosperity and in adversity. To prove this, I evidence those who recant on their deathbeds their previous unscrupulous devotion to temporal advantage.

124

If my dear love were but the child of state,
It might for Fortune's bastard be unfathered,
As subject to Time's love or to Time's hate,   3
Weeds among weeds, or flowers with flowers gathered.
No, it was builded far from accident;
It suffers not in smiling pomp, nor falls   6
Under the blow of thralled discontent,
Whereto the inviting time our fashion calls:
It fears not Policy, that heretic,   9
Which works on leases of short-numb'red hours,
But all alone stands hugely politic,
That it nor grows with heat nor drowns with show'rs.   12
    To this I witness call the fools of Time,
    Which die for goodness, who have lived for crime.

"Ever the same." From Octavio van Veen, *Amorum emblemata*
(1608). The verse reads:
    "When flowers are fresh and fair, we take in them delight;
    But faded once and done, all their esteem is past;
    Love does contrariwise in all times live and last,
    For Time must not bereave true love of due and right."

1. **Were't aught to me:** would it mean anything to me if; **canopy:** a covering held over the monarch's head in processions.

2. **extern:** visible self; **outward:** appearance.

3. **laid great bases for eternity:** aspired to win lasting fame by my praise of you.

4. **waste or ruining:** i.e., time required to destroy one's assets.

5. **form and favor:** handsome appearance.

8. **Pitiful thrivers:** prosperous ones who are ultimately to be pitied; **in their gazing spent:** used up in the act of looking.

9. **let me be obsequious in thy heart:** let my devotion be paid to your heart.

10. **oblation:** offering.

11. **seconds:** inferior adulterations; **art:** (1) skill; (2) artifice.

12. **render:** exchange.

13. **suborned informer:** conjectural false accuser.

⸻

What could I gain by paying formal homage to your external beauty, by public praise of it seeking to build a reputation that would last for eternity—an eternity that will not survive your beauty's destruction! Have I not seen those who emphasize external appearances ruined, offering elaborate compliments instead of honest appreciation, finally failing miserably to please because they spend all their efforts only on what they can see? No, let my homage be tendered to your heart, and take the offering of my love in exchange for yours. Away with all such false accusations; a constant lover is least affected by slander when most accused.

125

Were't aught to me I bore the canopy,
With my extern the outward honoring,
Or laid great bases for eternity,   3
Which proves more short than waste or ruining?
Have I not seen dwellers on form and favor
Lose all and more by paying too much rent,   6
For compound sweet forgoing simple savor,
Pitiful thrivers, in their gazing spent?
No, let me be obsequious in thy heart,   9
And take thou my oblation, poor but free,
Which is not mixed with seconds, knows no art
But mutual render, only me for thee.   12
   Hence, thou suborned informer! a true soul
    When most impeached stands least in thy control.

2. **glass:** mirror; **sickle hour:** possibly, the hour when his sickle is due to cut down. The Quarto has a comma after **sickle,** and some editors have conjectured that **hour** means hourglass.

3. **by waning grown:** grown in beauty even while aging.

6. **still:** ever; **pluck thee back:** hold back your alteration.

9. **minion:** (1) darling; (2) slave.

10. **still keep:** forever preserve.

11. **answered:** paid.

12. **quietus:** discharge; **render:** surrender.

⁕⁕⁕⁕⁕⁕⁕⁕⁕⁕⁕⁕⁕⁕⁕⁕⁕⁕⁕⁕⁕⁕⁕

You, my lovely boy, seem to be proof against Time's power to age your beauty and thereby show your lovers how they are themselves decaying. If it is Nature who keeps you unchanged, it can only be to spite Time. But beware of Nature, you who seem her darling but are really at her mercy! She may delay you but cannot preserve you forever: sooner or later she must close her account and surrender you to Time.

126

O thou, my lovely boy, who in thy power
Dost hold Time's fickle glass, his sickle hour;
Who hast by waning grown, and therein showst   3
Thy lovers withering as thy sweet self growst:
If Nature, sovereign mistress over wrack,
As thou goest onward, still will pluck thee back,   6
She keeps thee to this purpose, that her skill
May Time disgrace and wretched minutes kill.
Yet fear her, O thou minion of her pleasure!   9
She may detain, but not still keep, her treasure;
Her audit, though delayed, answered must be,
And her quietus is to render thee.   12

1. **In the old age:** formerly; **black:** (1) brunette hair and complexion; (2) ugliness.

2. **bore not beauty's name:** was at least not called beautiful.

3. **is black beauty's successive heir:** black (ugliness) inherits beauty's title.

4. **beauty slandered with a bastard shame:** true beauty is disinherited as illegitimate (artificial).

6. **Fairing the foul:** beautifying the ugly.

7. **Sweet:** natural; **name:** reputation; **holy bower:** sanctuary.

10. **so suited:** clothed to match.

12. **Sland'ring creation:** discrediting Nature's handiwork; **false esteem:** preference for the false.

13. **so they mourn, becoming of their woe:** they mourn so that their woe is attractive.

<hr>

Dark coloring once was not accounted beautiful, at least it was not so called; but now darkness is acknowledged to possess beauty, and beauty itself is called a counterfeit. For nowadays everyone has assumed Nature's power to create beauty from ugliness, and true beauty is no longer appreciated. Thus my mistress is brunette, with black eyes that seem to mourn because of the artificial beauty assumed by many, who prefer false styles and bring into disrepute the work of Nature. But her black eyes are so attractive in their mourning that everyone acclaims her as the model of beauty.

(Compare *Love's Labor's Lost,* IV.iii.286-93.)

127

In the old age black was not counted fair,
Or, if it were, it bore not beauty's name;
But now is black beauty's successive heir,   3
And beauty slandered with a bastard shame;
For since each hand hath put on Nature's power,
Fairing the foul with art's false borrowed face,   6
Sweet beauty hath no name, no holy bower,
But is profaned, if not lives in disgrace.
Therefore my mistress' brows are raven black,   9
Her eyes so suited, and they mourners seem
At such who, not born fair, no beauty lack,
Sland'ring creation with a false esteem: 12
    Yet so they mourn, becoming of their woe,
    That every tongue says beauty should look so.

2. **wood:** i.e., keys of the instrument, probably a virginal; **motion:** movement.

3. **swayst:** governest.

4. **wiry concord:** stringed harmony; **confounds:** overcomes.

5. **jacks:** apparently used for keys, but actually they were wooden uprights fitted with quills that plucked the strings of the instrument when the keys were pressed.

13. **jacks:** (1) keys; (2) rascals; **happy:** fortunate.

━━━━━━━━━━━━━━━━━━━━

How often when you, who are my music, play music on the keyboard, do I envy the keys that kiss your hand as you play! If mere wooden keys are allowed to be so presumptuous, give them your fingers, me your lips, to kiss.

128

How oft, when thou, my music, music playst,
Upon that blessed wood whose motion sounds
With thy sweet fingers when thou gently swayst   3
The wiry concord that mine ear confounds,
Do I envy those jacks that nimble leap
To kiss the tender inward of thy hand,   6
Whilst my poor lips, which should that harvest reap,
At the wood's boldness by thee blushing stand.
To be so tickled they would change their state   9
And situation with those dancing chips,
O'er whom thy fingers walk with gentle gait,
Making dead wood more blest than living lips.   12
    Since saucy jacks so happy are in this,
    Give them thy fingers, me thy lips, to kiss.

1. **spirit:** (1) spirituality; (2) bodily fluid (specifically, semen), or vitality; **waste of shame:** shameful waste.

3. **full of blame:** most worthy of condemnation.

4. **extreme:** violent; **rude:** brutal.

5. **straight:** at once.

6. **Past reason:** insanely.

11. **proof:** taste; **proved:** fully tried; **very:** mere.

14. **heaven:** bliss.

‖‖‖‖‖‖‖‖‖‖‖‖‖‖‖‖‖‖‖‖‖‖‖‖‖‖‖‖‖‖

A shameful waste of spirit and vitality results from the indulgence of lust; before consummation, lust can provoke lying, murder, and the most savage crimes; no sooner enjoyed than despised; sought with the passion of a madman and as madly hated when possessed; madness and violence attend every phase of it; a bliss to experience that leaves misery behind; a joy in prospect but afterward no more substantial than a dream. All know this well: but no one is wise enough to avoid the ecstasy that causes such pain.

129

The expense of spirit in a waste of shame
Is lust in action; and, till action, lust
Is perjured, murd'rous, bloody, full of blame, 3
Savage, extreme, rude, cruel, not to trust;
Enjoyed no sooner but despised straight;
Past reason hunted and, no sooner had, 6
Past reason hated as a swallowed bait,
On purpose laid to make the taker mad:
Mad in pursuit, and in possession so; 9
Had, having, and in quest to have, extreme;
A bliss in proof and, proved, a very woe;
Before, a joy proposed; behind, a dream. 12
  All this the world well knows; yet none knows well
  To shun the heaven that leads men to this hell.

4. **wires:** to which some other poets had compared their mistresses' hair.

5. **damasked:** patterned.

8. **reeks:** breathes (not necessarily unpleasantly).

11. **go:** walk.

13. **rare:** remarkable.

14. **she:** woman; **belied with false compare:** misrepresented with false comparisons.

⋯⋯⋯⋯⋯⋯⋯⋯⋯⋯⋯⋯

The extravagant comparisons used by other poets will not serve me to describe my mistress: she seems to me a woman endowed with ordinary beauty; but I swear I think her a match for any woman, no matter how elaborately poets may praise others.
(Compare No. 21.)

130

My mistress' eyes are nothing like the sun;
Coral is far more red than her lips' red;
If snow be white, why then her breasts are dun;   3
If hairs be wires, black wires grow on her head.
I have seen roses damasked, red and white,
But no such roses see I in her cheeks;   6
And in some perfumes is there more delight
Than in the breath that from my mistress reeks.
I love to hear her speak; yet well I know   9
That music hath a far more pleasing sound:
I grant I never saw a goddess go;
My mistress, when she walks, treads on the ground.   12
    And yet, by heaven, I think my love as rare
    As any she belied with false compare.

A literal portrait of a woman based on her lover's description.
From John Davies, *The Extravagant Shepherd* (1654). In the portrait, the artist gave the beloved mistress a complexion white as
snow, two branches of coral at the mouth opening, a lily and rose
for each cheek, two suns for eyes, and hair like chains of gold,
according to the text of Davies' "anti-romance."

1. **so:** just.
3. **dear:** fondly (intensifying **doting**).
10. **but:** only; **on:** of.
11. **on another's neck:** on top of another.
12. **in my judgment's place:** in my place of judgment.
13. **black:** foul, in the sense of "ugly."

᠁᠁᠁᠁᠁᠁᠁᠁᠁

Even though you are not beautiful, you treat me as capriciously as those whose pride in their beauty makes them cruel; you know how fondly I dote on you as my most beautiful treasure. Yet some sincerely say you are not fair enough to make a man groan with love; and I dare not contradict them, though privately I swear they are wrong. To prove my belief, I call to witness the many groans that the mere thought of your face inspires in me. Only your conduct is ugly; thence comes your disgrace.

131

Thou art as tyrannous, so as thou art,
As those whose beauties proudly make them cruel;
For well thou knowst to my dear, doting heart   3
Thou art the fairest and most precious jewel.
Yet in good faith some say that thee behold,
Thy face hath not the power to make love groan;   6
To say they err I dare not be so bold,
Although I swear it to myself alone.
And, to be sure that is not false I swear,   9
A thousand groans, but thinking on thy face,
One on another's neck, do witness bear
Thy black is fairest in my judgment's place.   12
  In nothing art thou black save in thy deeds,
    And thence this slander, as I think, proceeds.

4. **ruth:** pity.

7. **even:** evening.

10. **beseem:** seem appropriate to.

11. **doth thee grace:** becomes thee.

12. **suit:** dress; **like:** alike. The implication is that her heart is already black; it merely lacks the pity.

14. **foul:** (1) ugly; (2) unpleasant; **complexion:** secondary sense: disposition.

||||||||||||||||||||||||||||||||||||||

Your beloved eyes, black as they are, seem to pity my misery at your unkindness. Your eyes have the same splendid effect in your face as the rising sun or the evening star against the dull sky. Do, then, make your heart mourn for me, since mourning becomes you—your heart is already dressed to match your eyes. Then I'll avow that black is the pattern of beauty and that everyone is ugly (ill-tempered) that is not like you in coloring (disposition).

132

Thine eyes I love, and they, as pitying me,
Knowing thy heart torments me with disdain,
Have put on black and loving mourners be,   3
Looking with pretty ruth upon my pain.
And truly not the morning sun of heaven
Better becomes the gray cheeks of the east,   6
Nor that full star that ushers in the even
Doth half that glory to the sober west,
As those two mourning eyes become thy face.   9
Oh, let it then as well beseem thy heart
To mourn for me, since mourning doth thee grace,
And suit thy pity like in every part.   12
   Then will I swear beauty herself is black,
   And all they foul that thy complexion lack.

1. **Beshrew:** curse.
4. **slave to slavery:** the victim of infatuation.
6. **next self:** nearest self; the one dearest to my heart; **harder hast engrossed:** more firmly hast monopolized.
8. **crossed:** (1) frustrated; (2) crucified.
9. **ward:** prison.
10. **bail:** confine.
11. **keeps:** imprisons; **guard:** guardhouse.
14. **Perforce:** willy-nilly.

＿＿＿＿＿＿＿＿＿＿

Plague take the heart that causes mine such anguish for both my friend and myself! Is it not enough to torture me, without enslaving my dearest friend as well? You have divided me from my true self, and, even more cruelly, you have seized my friend; so that I have neither him, my self, nor you. Imprison my heart in that steely one of yours, but let my friend's heart be confined in mine; whoever safeguards me, let my heart be his prison; you will then be unable to treat him too cruelly. But you will after all; for I, being your prisoner, will act according to your hard heart.

133

Beshrew that heart that makes my heart to groan
For that deep wound it gives my friend and me:
Is't not enough to torture me alone   3
But slave to slavery my sweet'st friend must be?
Me from myself thy cruel eye hath taken,
And my next self thou harder hast engrossed;   6
Of him, myself, and thee I am forsaken,
A torment thrice threefold thus to be crossed.
Prison my heart in thy steel bosom's ward,   9
But then my friend's heart let my poor heart bail;
Whoe'er keeps me, let my heart be his guard:
Thou canst not then use rigor in my jail.   12
    And yet thou wilt; for I, being pent in thee,
    Perforce am thine, and all that is in me.

2. **mortgaged:** pledged; **will:** (1) wish; (2) lust.

5. **will not:** will not choose to be.

6. **covetous:** insatiable; **kind:** loving.

7. **surety-like:** i.e., as one acts as security for another's bond. Some think that Shakespeare had his noble friend intercede with the lady on his behalf.

8. **bond:** (1) contract; (2) tie of affection; **fast:** securely.

9. **The statute of thy beauty thou wilt take:** you will take full advantage of your beauty.

10. **use:** (1) profit; (2) sexual employment.

11. **came:** became.

12. **my unkind abuse:** my unnatural use of him.

⸻⸻⸻⸻⸻

Now that I have confessed that he is yours, and I am pledged to satisfy you, I will sacrifice my soul if you will release my other self. But you will not release him, and he will not wish to be released, because your appetite is insatiable and he is amorous; he acted at first for me but is now as firmly held by the bonds of love. And you will use your beauty for all it is worth—you who believe in making it profitable—and will make my friend redeem my insufficiency. Thus my abuse of friendship loses me my friend. I have lost him; you have both him and me; he fully pays you what I owe you; and yet I still must serve you.

134

So, now I have confessed that he is thine,
And I myself am mortgaged to thy will,
Myself I'll forfeit, so that other mine   3
Thou wilt restore to be my comfort still:
But thou wilt not, nor he will not be free,
For thou art covetous, and he is kind;   6
He learned but surety-like to write for me
Under that bond that him as fast doth bind.
The statute of thy beauty thou wilt take,   9
Thou usurer that putst forth all to use,
And sue a friend came debtor for my sake;
So him I lose through my unkind abuse.   12
   Him have I lost, thou hast both him and me;
   He pays the whole, and yet am I not free.

1. **Will:** (1) wish; (2) sexual appetite; (3) lover named **Will** (probably Shakespeare's friend). The two Wills in the next line are possibly the woman's husband and Shakespeare himself, who seems to be the extra **Will.** Compare also the proverb "Women will have their wills."

2. **to boot:** in addition.

6. **vouchsafe to hide my will in thine:** i.e., consent to yield your body to me.

7. **gracious:** attractive.

13. **no unkind, no fair beseechers kill:** some editors place one or the other **no** in quotation marks. There is probably some corruption in the line, but the sense is "do not kill any true suppliants with an unkind 'no.'"

14. **but:** only; **and me:** and count me.

⁙⁙⁙⁙⁙⁙⁙⁙⁙⁙⁙⁙⁙⁙⁙⁙⁙⁙⁙⁙⁙⁙⁙⁙⁙

You have a great appetite for pleasure and more than enough men to satisfy it. But must I be the one too many? If other men's desire attracts you, why should mine alone fail to please? The watery sea yet accepts the addition of rain; in the same way, accept this additional Will to add to your supply. Don't reject any honest suitor; consider all men only one man, and include me too.

135

Whoever hath her wish, thou hast thy Will,
And Will to boot, and Will in overplus.
More than enough am I that vex thee still,   3
To thy sweet will making addition thus.
Wilt thou, whose will is large and spacious,
Not once vouchsafe to hide my will in thine?   6
Shall will in others seem right gracious,
And in my will no fair acceptance shine?
The sea, all water, yet receives rain still   9
And in abundance addeth to his store;
So thou, being rich in Will, add to thy Will
One will of mine to make thy large Will more.   12
    Let no unkind, no fair beseechers kill;
    Think all but one, and me in that one Will.

1. **check:** rebuke; **come so near:** (1) speak so frankly; (2) become so intimate.

2. **thy Will:** some editors conjecture "Will, her husband."

3. **will . . . is admitted there:** i.e., (1) will is admitted as one of the constituents of the soul (the other being understanding); (2) your husband's intimacy is allowed.

4. **for love:** for love's sake.

5. **fulfill:** fill up; **treasure:** treasury.

7. **receipt:** capacity.

8. **one is reckoned none:** i.e., "One is no number"; compare No. 8, line 14.

9. **untold:** (1) uncounted; (2) unrevealed.

10. **your store's account:** (1) the total reckoning of your belongings; (2) your evaluation of your lovers.

11. **nothing:** secondary meaning: wicked; **hold:** account.

13. **my name:** i.e., will, in the senses used in the preceding sonnet.

‖‖‖‖‖‖‖‖‖‖‖‖‖‖‖‖‖‖‖‖‖‖‖‖‖‖‖

If your soul troubles you because of my intimacy with you, swear to it that I was your Will, an accepted intimate of your soul. Show enough affection to grant my lover's petition at least to this extent. This Will will complete your store of lovers—fill it up—one among many wills. One does not count among many; so let me go unacknowledged; count me nothing, so long as you cherish me at the same time. If you but continue to love your will, you love me, for my name is Will.

136

If thy soul check thee that I come so near,
Swear to thy blind soul that I was thy Will,
And will, thy soul knows, is admitted there: 3
Thus far for love my love-suit, sweet, fulfill.
Will will fulfill the treasure of thy love,
Ay, fill it full with wills, and my will one.   6
In things of great receipt with ease we prove,
Among a number one is reckoned none.
Then in the number let me pass untold,   9
Though in thy store's account I one must be;
For nothing hold me, so it please thee hold
That nothing me a something sweet to thee.   12
    Make but my name thy love, and love that still,
    And then thou lovest me, for my name is Will.

3. **lies:** (1) dwells; (2) deceives.

5. **corrupt:** seduced.

9. **several:** private.

12. **fair truth:** (1) true beauty; (2) fidelity of heart; **foul:** ugly.

14. **false plague:** plague of falseness.

⁣⁣⁣⁣⁣⁣⁣⁣⁣⁣⁣⁣⁣⁣⁣⁣⁣⁣⁣⁣⁣⁣⁣

Love, what are you doing to my eyes, that they can see without recognition? My eyes know true beauty, recognize its imitations, and yet accept the worst as though it were the best. If my eyes, seduced by fond glances, settle themselves upon a promiscuous woman, why have you caused my heart to follow my eyes? Why does my heart regard her as my private possession, when it knows she belongs to all? Or why do my eyes deny what they see, to make her appear faithful? My eyes and heart have denied what they knew as truth, and they are now afflicted with this falseness.

137

Thou blind fool, Love, what dost thou to mine eyes
That they behold and see not what they see?
They know what beauty is, see where it lies,   3
Yet what the best is take the worst to be.
If eyes, corrupt by overpartial looks,
Be anchored in the bay where all men ride,   6
Why of eyes' falsehood hast thou forged hooks,
Whereto the judgment of my heart is tied?
Why should my heart think that a several plot   9
Which my heart knows the wide world's common
    place?
Or mine eyes, seeing this, say this is not,
To put fair truth upon so foul a face?   12
  In things right true my heart and eyes have erred,
  And to this false plague are they now transferred.

(This poem was first printed by William Jaggard in 1599 in a collection of verse titled *The Passionate Pilgrim*, which Jaggard falsely attributed to Shakespeare's sole authorship. There are many variant readings in the version printed by Jaggard.)

    4. **subtilties:** deceptions.
    7. **Simply:** as though I were simple (innocent).
    8. **simple:** honest.
    9. **unjust:** dishonest, in the sense "unfaithful."
    11. **habit:** garb; **seeming:** (1) apparent; (2) becoming; **trust:** fidelity.
    12. **age:** an old man; **told:** counted.

When my mistress swears that she is wholly faithful, I believe her, though I know she lies; perhaps in this way she will think me an inexperienced youth, unacquainted with worldly deceptions. Thus foolishly believing that she thinks me young, although she knows better, with pretended innocence I believe her lying words; on both sides honesty is suppressed. Why does she not admit she is unfaithful? And why do I not say that I am old? Love appears to best advantage when it appears faithful; and an aged lover dislikes counting his years. Therefore we sleep together on false pretenses, and our flaws are glossed over with lies.

138

When my love swears that she is made of truth
I do believe her, though I know she lies,
That she might think me some untutored youth,   3
Unlearned in the world's false subtilties.
Thus vainly thinking that she thinks me young,
Although she knows my days are past the best,   6
Simply I credit her false-speaking tongue;
On both sides thus is simple truth suppressed.
But wherefore says she not she is unjust?   9
And wherefore say not I that I am old?
Oh, love's best habit is in seeming trust,
And age in love loves not to have years told.   12
  Therefore I lie with her and she with me,
  And in our faults by lies we flattered be.

3. **with thine eye:** i.e., by the way you look at another; **with thy tongue:** by frank confession.

4. **power with power:** your power with full force; **art:** stratagem.

8. **o'erpressed:** pressed beyond resistance; **bide:** endure.

10. **pretty:** wanton.

11. **foes:** i.e., her glances.

14. **Kill me outright with looks:** i.e., as the basilisk, a mythical reptile, was supposed to do; **rid:** destroy.

<hr />

Do not ask me to justify the pain your infidelity causes me! Wound me not by ogling others but by speech; use your full power, and do not kill me with subtle slowness. Tell me you love another; but do not look lovingly at another in my presence. But I will excuse you thus for doing so: Ah, my love knows that her amorous looks have harmed me; and therefore she turns her glances away from me to do mischief elsewhere. But please do not; since I am nearly dead already, kill me outright with your basilisk glance and free me from pain.

139

Oh, call not me to justify the wrong
That thy unkindness lays upon my heart;
Wound me not with thine eye but with thy tongue;   3
Use power with power, and slay me not by art.
Tell me thou lovest elsewhere; but in my sight,
Dear heart, forbear to glance thine eye aside;   6
What needst thou wound with cunning when thy
    might
Is more than my o'erpressed defense can bide?
Let me excuse thee: ah, my love well knows   9
Her pretty looks have been mine enemies;
And therefore from my face she turns my foes,
That they elsewhere might dart their injuries: 12
   Yet do not so; but since I am near slain,
    Kill me outright with looks and rid my pain.

1. **press:** oppress.
4. **pity-wanting:** pity-lacking; unpitied.
5. **wit:** wisdom.
11. **ill-wresting:** given to evil interpretation.
13. **That:** so that.
14. **straight:** incorporating the sense "strait" (narrowly); **proud:** lustful; **wide:** astray.

||||||||||||||||||||||||||||||||||||||

In your cruelty, show equal wisdom; do not try my patience too far, lest I find words to express the pitiless way in which you torture me. You would be wise, even if you do not love me, to tell me that you do; just as the irritable sick man is assured by his doctor that he is well. If I despair, I shall be mad and in my mad ravings may speak ill of you; and the world today is so quick to distort everything to evil that even a madman's words would be believed. So that I may not be mad and slander you, direct your glances strictly at me, although your lustful heart may be attracted elsewhere.

140

Be wise as thou art cruel: do not press
My tongue-tied patience with too much disdain,
Lest sorrow lend me words and words express   3
The manner of my pity-wanting pain.
If I might teach thee wit, better it were,
Though not to love, yet, love, to tell me so;   6
As testy sick men, when their deaths be near,
No news but health from their physicians know.
For if I should despair, I should grow mad,   9
And in my madness might speak ill of thee:
Now this ill-wresting world is grown so bad,
Mad slanderers by mad ears believed be.   12
  That I may not be so, nor thou belied,
    Bear thine eyes straight, though thy proud heart
      go wide.

2. **errors:** flaws (probably both moral and physical).

4. **despite:** spite; **view:** appearance.

6. **tender feeling:** sensitivity; **base touches:** (1) coarse-textured objects of touch; (2) contacts with baseness.

8. **alone:** only (of all women).

9. **wits:** common wit, imagination, fantasy, estimation, and memory, according to Stephen Hawes, a writer of the early sixteenth century

11. **Who:** which (the heart); **unswayed:** ungoverned; **the likeness of a man:** i.e., one who resembles a man but is less than human, lacking his heart.

14. **pain:** punishment; i.e., so that he performs penance even as he sins.

▬▬▬▬▬▬▬▬▬▬

Truly, my eyes are not responsible for my loving you, for they observe your many faults; 'tis my heart that dotes on you, despite the evidence of my eyes. My ears are not thrilled by your speech, nor my delicacy attracted to your coarseness; neither my taste nor smell are attracted to you beyond all other women. But my wits and my senses cannot win my heart from its allegiance to you, so that my body is left unruled while my heart acts as your slave. But this love that afflicts me is at least to my advantage in that she who causes me to sin punishes me for it simultaneously.

141

In faith, I do not love thee with mine eyes,
For they in thee a thousand errors note;
But 'tis my heart that loves what they despise,   3
Who in despite of view is pleased to dote.
Nor are mine ears with thy tongue's tune delighted,
Nor tender feeling to base touches prone,   6
Nor taste nor smell desire to be invited
To any sensual feast with thee alone.
But my five wits nor my five senses can   9
Dissuade one foolish heart from serving thee,
Who leaves unswayed the likeness of a man,
Thy proud heart's slave and vassal wretch to be: 12
    Only my plague thus far I count my gain,
    That she that makes me sin awards me pain.

2. **grounded on sinful loving:** based on the fact that my love is sinful because adulterous.

8. **Robbed others' beds' revenues of their rents:** i.e., committed adultery.

9. **Be it:** regard it as.

12. **Thy pity may deserve to pitied be:** your pity will earn pity for yourself.

13. **hide:** deny.

⁓⁓⁓⁓⁓⁓⁓⁓⁓⁓⁓⁓⁓⁓⁓⁓⁓⁓⁓⁓⁓⁓⁓

My sin is love, your virtue hate, hate of what you call my sin in loving you adulterously. But only compare my condition with your own and you will realize that mine does not deserve reproach—or if it does, not from your lips, that have breathed illegal vows of love as often as I and have fostered adultery. Only consider that my love for you is as lawful as yours for those whom you lure, even while my eyes plead with you: raise some pity in your heart, that you may earn pity for yourself when you need it. If you seek pity yourself, having denied it, you may be refused.

142

Love is my sin, and thy dear virtue hate,
Hate of my sin, grounded on sinful loving.
Oh, but with mine compare thou thine own state, 3
And thou shalt find it merits not reproving;
Or if it do, not from those lips of thine,
That have profaned their scarlet ornaments 6
And sealed false bonds of love as oft as mine,
Robbed others' beds' revenues of their rents.
Be it lawful I love thee as thou lovest those 9
Whom thine eyes woo as mine importune thee:
Root pity in thy heart, that, when it grows,
Thy pity may deserve to pitied be. 12
   If thou dost seek to have what thou dost hide,
   By self-example mayst thou be denied.

1. **Lo as:** just as; **careful:** anxious.

3. **dispatch:** haste.

8. **prizing:** taking account of; **discontent:** unhappiness.

11. **hope:** object hoped for.

13. **Will:** the same potential meanings as in No. 135.

░░░░░░░░░░░░░░░░░░░░░░░░░░

Just as an anxious housewife runs after a runaway fowl, putting down her infant and speeding in pursuit, while the babe chases after and cries at her lack of attention; just so do you run after a man that runs from you, while I, your child, chase you; if you get what you want, give me your attention again, kiss me lovingly. I will pray that you gain your Will, on condition that you give this Will what he cries for too.

143

Lo as a careful housewife runs to catch
One of her feathered creatures broke away,
Sets down her babe, and makes all swift dispatch   3
In pursuit of the thing she would have stay;
Whilst her neglected child holds her in chase,
Cries to catch her whose busy care is bent   6
To follow that which flies before her face,
Not prizing her poor infant's discontent:
So runnst thou after that which flies from thee,   9
Whilst I, thy babe, chase thee afar behind;
But if thou catch thy hope, turn back to me
And play the mother's part, kiss me, be kind.   12
   So will I pray that thou mayst have thy Will,
   If thou turn back and my loud crying still.

(This sonnet also appeared in Jaggard's *Passionate Pilgrim* [1599].)

2. **suggest:** prompt.
4. **colored ill:** i.e., dark.
8. **pride:** sexuality.
10. **directly:** (1) at once; (2) completely.
11. **from:** absent from; **both to each friend:** each being a lover of the other.
12. **hell:** the sexual meaning is fairly obvious.
14. **fire . . . out:** infect with venereal disease.

‖‖‖‖‖‖‖‖‖‖‖‖‖‖‖‖‖‖‖‖‖‖‖‖‖‖‖‖‖‖‖‖

I have two loves, one offering spiritual solace, the other despair, and, like good and evil angels, they move my soul. The better angel is a fair man, the worser a dark woman. To give me an early taste of hell, my female evil tempts away my better angel, seeking to corrupt him with her appetite. I suspect that my angel has fallen, though I cannot say so positively; but since both are away from me and they attract each other, I guess they have become lovers. But I shall not know this until my bad angel infects my good one with venereal disease.

144

Two loves I have, of comfort and despair,
Which like two spirits do suggest me still:
The better angel is a man right fair,   3
The worser spirit a woman colored ill.
To win me soon to hell, my female evil
Tempteth my better angel from my side,   6
And would corrupt my saint to be a devil,
Wooing his purity with her foul pride.
And whether that my angel be turned fiend,   9
Suspect I may, yet not directly tell;
But being both from me, both to each friend,
I guess one angel in another's hell.   12
   Yet this shall I ne'er know, but live in doubt,
   Till my bad angel fire my good one out.

(Fairly general doubt exists as to Shakespeare's authorship of this sonnet because of its triviality and its lack of coherence with the others that concern a woman. It is certainly one of the few that the woman in question could have seen without being offended.)

5. **Straight:** immediately.
7. **used in:** accustomed to; **doom:** judgment.

‖‖‖‖‖‖‖‖‖‖‖‖‖‖‖‖‖‖‖‖‖‖‖‖‖‖‖

My mistress' lips, shaped by Love's own hand, formed for me, her pining lover, the words "I hate," but when she saw my wretchedness, her merciful heart changed her tongue to its customary mildness and added a gentle end to her greeting: she annulled the words "I hate" by adding "not you."

145

Those lips that Love's own hand did make
Breathed forth the sound that said "I hate"
To me that languished for her sake;   3
But when she saw my woeful state,
Straight in her heart did mercy come,
Chiding that tongue that ever sweet   6
Was used in giving gentle doom,
And taught it thus anew to greet:
"I hate" she altered with an end   9
That followed it as gentle day
Doth follow night, who, like a fiend,
From heaven to hell is flown away.   12
  "I hate" from hate away she threw,
  And saved my life, saying, "not you."

1. **earth:** body.

2. **Foiled by:** (1) defeated by; (2) defiled by. This is an emendation first suggested by a nineteenth-century editor; the Quarto repeats the words "My sinful earth"; **array:** (1) envelop; (2) disfigure.

4. **so costly gay:** i.e., with such expensive magnificence.

7. **excess:** extravagance.

8. **charge:** body (on which so much has been spent).

9. **thy servant's loss:** i.e., the body's destruction.

10. **aggravate:** increase.

11. **terms divine:** eternal life; **hours of dross:** transitory rubbish.

My poor soul, why do you endure starvation, while the body that envelops you is decked in costly finery? Why so much expense to clothe your body, which lasts so short a time? Shall worms, your ultimate owners, consume this outlay? Is this the end for which your body was created? If so, do you feed upon your body's destruction; let it starve while you increase in strength; gain eternity by selling ephemeral trash; feed yourself, while your body goes unadorned. Thus, by consuming Death's prey, the body, you will devour Death himself and live eternally.

146

Poor soul, the center of my sinful earth,
[Foiled by] these rebel pow'rs that thee array,
Why dost thou pine within and suffer dearth,   3
Painting thy outward walls so costly gay?
Why so large cost, having so short a lease,
Dost thou upon thy fading mansion spend?   6
Shall worms, inheritors of this excess,
Eat up thy charge? Is this thy body's end?
Then, soul, live thou upon thy servant's loss,   9
And let that pine to aggravate thy store;
Buy terms divine in selling hours of dross;
Within be fed, without be rich no more: 12
   So shalt thou feed on Death, that feeds on men,
   And Death once dead, there's no more dying then.

2. **nurseth:** nourishes.

3. **ill:** ailment.

4. **uncertain:** fickle.

7. **desperate:** hopelessly ill; **approve:** demonstrate.

8. **physic did except:** rejected medicine.

9. **Past cure . . . past care:** proverbial, though the sense of the proverb is that there is no use in worrying about a hopeless case; here, the meaning is that a cure is impossible once the doctor has ceased to care for the patient.

12. **At random from:** wide of; **vainly:** nonsensically.

‖‖‖‖‖‖‖‖‖‖‖‖‖‖‖‖‖‖‖‖‖‖‖‖

My love, like a fever, keeps me yearning continually for possession of the woman, which only increases my passion. My reason has deserted me, since I gave no heed to its advice, and my desperate case proves that insatiable desire is fatal. I cannot be cured since I am no longer attended by reason, and unresting desire drives me mad; both my thoughts and my speech resemble a madman's in their unreality and lack of sense: for I have sworn that you are fair and lovely and thought you pure, when you are as evil as hell and as dark as night.

147

My love is as a fever, longing still
For that which longer nurseth the disease,
Feeding on that which doth preserve the ill,   3
The uncertain sickly appetite to please.
My reason, the physician to my love,
Angry that his prescriptions are not kept,   6
Hath left me, and I desperate now approve
Desire is death, which physic did except.
Past cure I am, now reason is past care,   9
And frantic-mad with evermore unrest;
My thoughts and my discourse as madmen's are,
At random from the truth, vainly expressed: 12
   For I have sworn thee fair, and thought thee bright,
   Who art as black as hell, as dark as night.

"Love refuseth help." From Octavio van Veen, *Amorum emblemata*
(1608). The verse reads:
   "Love lying sick in bed rejecteth physic's skill;
     The cause of all his grief it grieves him to remove;
     He knows love works his grief, yet will not leave to love;
     No reason nor no herb can then recure his ill."

4. **censures:** judges.

5. **fair:** (1) beautiful; (2) true; **false:** deceiving.

7. **denote:** signify.

10. **watching:** lack of sleep.

11. **though:** if; **mistake my view:** misinterpret what I see.

13. **love:** here addressing the mistress, not the emotion nor the god.

⎪⎪⎪⎪⎪⎪⎪⎪⎪⎪⎪⎪⎪⎪⎪⎪⎪⎪⎪⎪⎪⎪⎪⎪⎪⎪⎪⎪⎪⎪⎪⎪⎪

Alas, how love has affected my eyes, that what they see does not accord with reality! or, if it does, where is my judgment, that it contradicts what my eyes see truly? If my untrustworthy eyes dote on what is truly fair, why does the world say otherwise? If not truly fair, then love clearly indicates that love's eye is not as honest as everyone else's. But how can love's eye be true when lack of sleep and tears oppress it? It is no wonder that I misunderstand what I see; even the sun's eye is dimmed by cloud. O crafty mistress, you blind me with tears at your cruelty, lest healthy vision detect your faults!

148

Oh, me! what eyes hath love put in my head,
Which have no correspondence with true sight;
Or, if they have, where is my judgment fled,   3
That censures falsely what they see aright?
If that be fair whereon my false eyes dote,
What means the world to say it is not so?   6
If it be not, then love doth well denote
Love's eye is not so true as all men's: no,
How can it? Oh, how can Love's eye be true,   9
That is so vexed with watching and with tears?
No marvel then though I mistake my view:
The sun itself sees not till heaven clears.   12
    O cunning love, with tears thou keepst me blind,
    Lest eyes well seeing thy foul faults should find.

2. **partake:** take part; side.

3. **on:** of; **forgot:** forgotten.

4. **all tyrant:** self-punisher.

7. **lowrst:** frown; **spend:** employ.

8. **present moan:** immediate pain.

9. **respect:** take note of.

11. **defect:** i.e., downright deficiency, moral and physical.

12. **motion:** prompting.

||||||||||||||||||||||||||||||||||||

How can you, cruel one, say I do not love you, when I side with you against myself? Do not I think of you, completely forgetting my own interests? If you look at me hostilely, do not I punish myself as your enemy with immediate pain? In what way do I seem to think myself too good to serve you, when your mere glance inspires my adoration of you, imperfect as you are? But, my love, hate on; for now I understand your reasoning: you love those who can see, and my worship of you proves that I am blind.

149

Canst thou, O cruel! say I love thee not,
When I against myself with thee partake?
Do I not think on thee when I forgot   3
Am of myself, all tyrant for thy sake?
Who hateth thee that I do call my friend?
On whom frownst thou that I do fawn upon?   6
Nay, if thou lowrst on me, do I not spend
Revenge upon myself with present moan?
What merit do I in myself respect   9
That is so proud thy service to despise,
When all my best doth worship thy defect,
Commanded by the motion of thine eyes?   12
   But, love, hate on, for now I know thy mind:
    Those that can see thou lovest, and I am blind.

2. **insufficiency:** defectiveness.

3. **give the lie to:** contradict.

4. **brightness doth not grace the day:** i.e., that darkness rather than brightness becomes the day.

5. **becoming of things ill:** gracing of evil.

6. **the very refuse of thy deeds:** thy basest actions.

7. **strength and warrantise of skill:** i.e., strong sanction in the skill with which you act.

⁕⁕⁕⁕⁕⁕⁕⁕⁕⁕⁕⁕⁕⁕⁕⁕⁕⁕⁕⁕⁕⁕⁕⁕⁕

Whence do you derive this power to rule my heart with your very faults, causing me to contradict the evidence of my sight and swear that your dark self better becomes the day than does the sun? Whence have you this power to grace evil, so that your worst actions seem excused by your skill in performance and surpass the best deeds of others? Whence have you learned to make me love you more, the more I have reason to hate you? Even if I love what others hate, you should not hate me for loving you: if I can love your unworthy self, I am the more worthy of your love.

150

Oh, from what pow'r hast thou this pow'rful might,
With insufficiency my heart to sway?
To make me give the lie to my true sight,   3
And swear that brightness doth not grace the day?
Whence hast thou this becoming of things ill,
That in the very refuse of thy deeds   6
There is such strength and warrantise of skill
That in my mind thy worst all best exceeds?
Who taught thee how to make me love thee more,   9
The more I hear and see just cause of hate?
Oh, though I love what others do abhor,
With others thou shouldst not abhor my state: 12
    If thy unworthiness raised love in me,
    More worthy I to be beloved of thee.

1. **Love:** i.e., the love-god; **conscience:** secondary sense: carnal knowledge.

3. **urge not my amiss:** do not stress my sin.

10. **triumphant:** spectacular; **Proud of this pride:** (flesh) swelling with sexual excitement.

||||||||||||||||||||||||||||||||||||

The poet here blames the dark lady for his bondage to physical passion.

151

Love is too young to know what conscience is;
Yet who knows not conscience is born of love?
Then, gentle cheater, urge not my amiss,   3
Lest guilty of my faults thy sweet self prove.
For, thou betraying me, I do betray
My nobler part to my gross body's treason;   6
My soul doth tell my body that he may
Triumph in love; flesh stays no farther reason,
But, rising at thy name, doth point out thee   9
As his triumphant prize. Proud of this pride,
He is contented thy poor drudge to be,
To stand in thy affairs, fall by thy side.   12
    No want of conscience hold it that I call
    Her "love" for whose dear love I rise and fall.

1. **am forsworn:** have broken my marriage vow.
3. **faith:** vow of fidelity.
7. **misuse:** deceive.
8. **all my honest faith in thee is lost:** i.e., my dealings with you have completely corrupted my honesty.
11. **enlighten thee:** make you fairer; **give eyes to blindness:** described things I was unable to see.
13. **eye:** pun on "I."

|||||||||||||||||||||||||||||||||||||||

You know I have broken my marriage vow in loving you; but you are twice an oath-breaker, in both violating your marriage pledge and annulling your faith to me by a new vow of hate soon after your vow of love. But why should I accuse you of two breaches of your oath, when I have broken so many? All my vows for your sake were deceptions, and I have no integrity left. For I have sworn oaths of your virtue, love, and constancy; and to flatter you I have sworn to things I never saw and denied the true sight of my eyes. For I have sworn that you are fair and true: all the more am I perjured, swearing so black a lie!

152

In loving thee thou knowst I am forsworn,
But thou art twice forsworn, to me love swearing;
In act thy bed-vow broke, and new faith torn   3
In vowing new hate after new love bearing.
But why of two oaths' breach do I accuse thee,
When I break twenty? I am perjured most,   6
For all my vows are oaths but to misuse thee,
And all my honest faith in thee is lost;
For I have sworn deep oaths of thy deep kindness,   9
Oaths of thy love, thy truth, thy constancy,
And, to enlighten thee, gave eyes to blindness,
Or made them swear against the thing they see.   12
   For I have sworn thee fair: more perjured eye,
   To swear against the truth so foul a lie.

(This and No. 154 seem to be based at some remove on a poem by Marianus Scholasticus in the *Greek Anthology* [9.627]. The "conceit" of the two sonnets was used by many writers of the Renaissance; Shakespeare's immediate source has not been established.)

1. **brand:** torch.
2. **maid of Dian's:** i.e., a nymph, who as a follower of Diana, the chaste moon-goddess, was dedicated to chastity; **advantage:** opportunity.
6. **dateless:** unending; **still:** ever.
7. **seething:** boiling.
8. **strange:** extreme; **sovereign:** peerless.
11. **bath:** capitalized by some editors to specify the hot springs at Bath, Somerset, but there were other medicinal springs in England, and Bath had no special prominence in Shakespeare's time.
12. **sad distempered:** miserably ill.

<hr>

Cupid lay down to sleep, his torch beside him: one of Diana's nymphs took the opportunity to quench his love-kindling fire in a nearby fountain, which acquired an eternal heat from Love's fire and became a boiling bath that men still find peerless for serious ailments. But Love refired his torch from my mistress' eye and tested it on my heart; sick with love therefrom, I sped to that bath but found no cure: my only help lies in the source of Cupid's fire, my mistress' eye.

153

Cupid laid by his brand and fell asleep:
A maid of Dian's this advantage found
And his love-kindling fire did quickly steep   3
In a cold valley fountain of that ground;
Which borrowed from this holy fire of Love
A dateless lively heat, still to endure,   6
And grew a seething bath, which yet men prove
Against strange maladies a sovereign cure.
But at my mistress' eye Love's brand new-fired,   9
The boy for trial needs would touch my breast;
I, sick withal, the help of bath desired
And thither hied, a sad distempered guest,   12
    But found no cure, the bath for my help lies
    Where Cupid got new fire, my mistress' eyes.

"Love is love's physician." From Octavio van Veen, *Amorum
emblemata* (1608). The verse reads:
  "By whom the harm is wrought, the remedy is found;
   The causer of the smart is causer of the ease;
   He cures the sickness best that caused the disease;
   Love must the plaster lay where love hath made the wound."

(This sonnet employs the same theme as the preceding one, with a slight variation in the ending.)

7. **general:** commander.
9. **by:** nearby.

||||||||||||||||||||||||||||||||||||||||||||

To sleep, the love-god laid his torch beside him; one of a group of nymphs dedicated to chaste life seized the torch and quenched it in a nearby well, which was given eternal heat from Love's fire and became a medicinal bath. But I came there seeking relief from the passion with which my mistress enslaves me and found this: Love's fire heats water; water cools not love.

154

The little love-god, lying once asleep,
Laid by his side his heart-inflaming brand,
Whilst many nymphs that vowed chaste life to keep   3
Came tripping by; but in her maiden hand
The fairest votary took up that fire,
Which many legions of true hearts had warmed;   6
And so the general of hot desire
Was, sleeping, by a virgin hand disarmed.
This brand she quenched in a cool well by,   9
Which from Love's fire took heat perpetual,
Growing a bath and healthful remedy
For men diseased; but I, my mistress' thrall,   12
    Came there for cure, and this by that I prove:
    Love's fire heats water; water cools not love.

"Love's fire is unquenchable." From Octavio van Veen, *Amorum
emblemata* (1608). The verse reads:
    "No water slakes Love's heat but makes his fire to flame;
    Cupid's heart-burning fire makes water for to burn.
    By coldness he doth cause increasing heat's return;
    Where Love hath hope of help, his harm lies in the same."

Index of First Lines

Index of First Lines

Index of First Lines

Index of First Lines

Index of First Lines